Read It Again!
Standards-Based Literature Lessons for Young Children

by Linda Ayers
Concepts for Artwork by Linda Ayers

Linworth
PUBLISHING, INC

I dedicate this book to my mother, Esther Williams,
and the memory of my grandmother, Gladys Cole,
two strong women who taught me that stubborn-
ness could be a virtue.

Copyright © 2003 by Linda Ayers

Library of Congress Cataloging-in-Publication Data

Ayers, Linda.
    Lively literature activities : standards-based literature lessons for
young children / by Linda Ayers.
        p. cm.
    Includes bibliographical references.
    ISBN 1-58683-123-2 (pbk.)
    1. School libraries--Activity programs. 2. Education,
Primary--Activity programs. 3. Education, Preschool--Activity programs.
    4. Early childhood education--Activity programs. 5. Children--Books
and reading. I. Title.
    Z675.S3A94 2003
    027.8'222--dc21

                                                    2003007931

Editor: Cindy Barden
Design and Production: Good Neighbor Press, Inc., Grand Junction, Colorado 81503

Published by Linworth Publishing, Inc.
480 East Wilson Bridge Road, Suite L
Worthington, Ohio 43085

ISBN: 1-58683-072-4

5 4 3 2 1

Table of Contents

JUV
591
F59i

JUV
W225mc

JUV
513.2
B167q

JUV
K25s
c.1-9

JUV
Sl62t

JUV
T124wh

Chapter III: Early Elementary III

Acknowledgments

A writer may put words on paper in isolation, but the community of friends, family, and associates makes the dream come true. Thanks to my family for their patience and pats on the back. To my husband, Bill, for taking care of the home front, offering suggestions, and being such a vital part of this book by photographing goat puppets and silly snakes as if they were fine art. To my son, Ryan, whose computer wizardry bailed me out more than once. To my son, Ben, for trying out activities and cheering me across the finish line.

Thanks to all my friends who have given suggestions, encouragement, and time. A special thanks to Jane for giving me a quiet place to work, to Sherry for her continual support when I needed it most, to Herb for getting me started, to Janice for encouraging me professionally, to Steve for giving me a chance to share the activities with public librarians, to Denise for sharing her expertise, to Doty for reading sample chapters with a teacher's eye, to Dana for listening with the ear of a writer and teacher, and to Jeremy and Judy for helping me over the final hurdle.

A special thanks to the Mabank ISD administrators, librarians, and staff for their support, and to the Central Elementary students for making my job as a librarian such a joy. To the Linworth reviewers for giving their professional opinions and helping me stay on track. To the Linworth team, especially Marlene Woo-Lun, and my editor, Donna Miller, for helping make this book the best it could be and showing an inordinate amount of patience.

Welcome to Read It Again!

Standards-Based Literature Lessons for Young Children

Reading to children from an early age remains one of the best ways to create independent readers. Storytime may seem difficult to justify when there are state and national education standards to meet, circulation figures to maintain, and technology skills to develop. Yet, this vital activity can teach skills that reinforce education standards, complement what is being taught in the classroom, and serve as a springboard to technology skills. The pure pleasure in reading will translate, over the long term, into increased circulation and a new generation of readers.

There is something in *Read It Again!* for everyone who works with children. The wide variety of storytime activities will fit into any schedule. Activities with no preparation time are balanced with those detailed projects that can be used over and over again. *Read It Again!* can rejuvenate storytime and serve as a benchmark for educational standards.

The titles in *Read It Again!* will appeal to preschool, kindergarten and early elementary children. All titles included in this work, both old standbys and recent publications, have received positive reviews. There are activities for those special, timeless books as well as for books that are destined to become new favorites. A bibliography is included to assist in collection development.

The emphasis of *Read It Again!* is on literature supported by successful, developmentally appropriate activities that librarians can easily adapt to fit their needs. The most effective library programs include collaboration with classroom teachers and/or parents. Many of the activities in *Read It Again!* can be used in the classroom or even at home, making it easy to encourage collaboration.

The Skills Table at the beginning of each story is a quick reference guide that summarizes each activity. The table is designed to assist the librarian in making title and activity selections and save valuable time. Each table includes:

- A summary of each picture book
- Activity name
- Preparation time
- Activity time
- Skills and matching standards
- Setting recommendations (library, classroom or home)

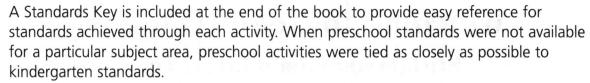

A Standards Key is included at the end of the book to provide easy reference for standards achieved through each activity. When preschool standards were not available for a particular subject area, preschool activities were tied as closely as possible to kindergarten standards.

The many enjoyable and curriculum-based activities include a summary, supply list, preparation notes, discussion section and activity steps. In addition to featuring timesaving reproducibles, the activities provide a range of preparation times. Some projects can be created and used many times. Most activities can be easily modified to fit a specific setting or curriculum need.

Many activities include Tech Tie-Ins. Although computers and the Internet cannot replace hands-on experiences for young children, they are essential for enriching today's curriculum and for providing experiences not available any other way. The Tech Tie-In feature is also an effective way to extend storytime into the classroom and home setting.

All Tech Tie-In software, videos, cassette tapes and CDs have received favorable reviews, and the Web sites have been selected using American Library Association guidelines. Just as the librarian or teacher should read any book before sharing it with children, all users of this book are strongly advised to check Web sites before planning any activities. A listing of Web sites organized by book title is included to simplify this process.

Hello, Shoes!

by Joan Blos

Blos, Joan, *Hello, Shoes!* Simon and Schuster Books for Young Readers, 1999, 24 pp., 0-689-81441-0

Follow a little boy and his grandfather as they look all over the house for the little boy's favorite shoes. When the little boy finally finds his shoes and then succeeds in buckling them for the very first time, the grandfather shows his pride by singing a song about the little boy buckling his shoes so early in the morning. This gentle story is wonderful for showing a nontraditional, loving family.

◆ Skills Table ◆

Activity	Time	Location	Subjects	Skills	Standards
Mix and Match	P: 20 min. A: 15 min.	C, L	Math	Number relationships; classifying objects	NCTM 1, 2
			Language Arts	Communicate effectively	NCTE 4
Skip in Your Shoes	P: none A: 10 min.	C, H, L	Dance	Skipping; using dance to communicate	MENC D-1, D-3
			Music	Sing in groups	MENC M-1

P: Approximate Preparation Time   **A:** Approximate Activity Time   **C:** Classroom Activity
H: Home Activity   **L:** Library Activity

Mix and Match

Children can match these mixed-up shoes with their own. The silliness begins when the shoes carry on a conversation!

Supplies:

◆ Two copies of each shoe reproducible

◆ Crayons or markers

Preparation:

◆ Make two copies of each shoe reproducible so that you have four pairs of shoes.

◆ Color each pair, making sure to color two different pairs of shoes the same color so that children learn to identify pairs by details other than color.

◆ Cut out shoes and laminate.

Discussion:

(Ask after reading the book to the children.)

Show the illustrations from the book that include the little boy's sandals. Point out that his sandals are called a pair of shoes because they match. Have the children look at the shoes they are wearing.

> Do your shoes match?

> Are they a pair?

Show the children the shoe reproducibles. Hold up a matching pair of shoes.

> Is this a pair of shoes?

> How are they alike?

Hold up two shoes that do not match and are different colors.

> Is this a pair of shoes?

> How are they different?

> Are they alike in any way?

> How would you look if you wore these two shoes together?

Hold up two shoes that do not match but are the same color.

> Is this a pair of shoes?
>
> How are they different?
>
> What else comes in pairs? *(mittens, socks)*

Activity:

1. Have four children stand in front of the group. Give each one a different shoe picture.

2. Discuss the different shoes. How do they fasten? What color is the shoe?

3. Pass out the remaining shoe pictures to four other children. Ask them to find the shoe that matches the one they are holding.

4. When they find it, they should stand next to the person with the matching shoe.

5. When everyone has found their matching shoe, tell the children that the shoes are now going to carry on a silly conversation.

6. Show the children how to carry on a shoe conversation by standing next to one of the teams. Point to each of the talking shoes as you say:

   Shoe 1: Hi, partner.

   Shoe 2: I'm glad I found you!

   Shoe 1: Aren't we a pair!

   Shoe 2: We belong together.

7. Have the children take turns with their silly shoe conversation.

8. Repeat the activity until all the children have had a turn.

Shoe Reproducibles

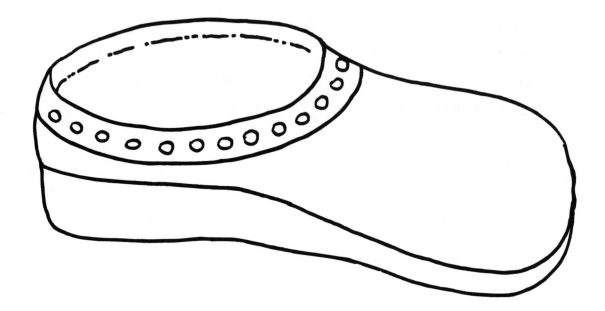

Shoe Reproducibles

Skip in Your Shoes

Skip around the room with this version of "Skip To My Lou." Children can practice ways to fasten their shoes, then they're off and skipping again.

Supplies:

◆ None

Preparation:

◆ None

Discussion:

Have children look at their shoes.

How many of you have shoes that buckle?

Ask the children to pretend to buckle their shoes.

Continue asking the children to identify their types of fasteners: tie, slip on, zipper, or Velcro®, and have them pantomime fastening each type of shoe.

Do you ever have to stop and tie your shoe (or have someone tie it for you) when you are walking somewhere?

Activity:

1. Show the children how to skip. (Very young children may walk instead of skipping.)

2. Tell the children they are going to play a skipping game where everyone skips around the room. When you stop skipping, everyone will stop and pretend to fasten their shoes before they begin to skip again. Each time they stop, they will pretend to fasten a different kind of shoe.

3. Have the children stand in a single-file line. Lead them as they skip around the room while everyone sings the song. Continue until every type of shoe worn by the children has been pantomimed.

Sing this song to the tune of *Skip To My Lou*. Repeat the refrain after each verse. Add other actions according to the kinds of shoes the children are wearing. Are there children with shoes that zip or have Velcro® fasteners? Add verses to sing about them.

Skip in Your Shoes

Refrain: Skip, skip, skip in your shoes
Skip, skip, skip in your shoes
Skip, skip, skip in your shoes
Skip in your shoes my darling.

1. Tie your shoe,
   I will too,
   Tie your shoe,
   I will too,
   Tie your shoe,
   I will too,
   Skip in your shoes my darling.

   Refrain

2. Buckle your shoe,
   I will too,
   Buckle your shoe,
   I will too,
   Buckle your shoe,
   I will too,
   Skip in your shoes my darling.

   Refrain

3. Slip on your shoe,
   I will too,
   Slip on your shoe,
   I will too,
   Slip on your shoe,
   I will too,
   Skip in your shoes my darling.

Here Comes Mother Goose

Edited by Iona Opie

Here Comes Mother Goose. Edited by Iona Opie.
Candlewick Press, 1999, 107 pp., 0-7636-0683-9

This second Mother Goose book with the winning team of Iona Opie and Rosemary Wells is just as delightful as their first collaboration, *My Very First Mother Goose*. An index of first lines makes it easy to find just what you're looking for, and the large colorful illustrations make this a great book to share at storytime.

◆ Skills Table ◆

Activity	Time	Location	Subjects	Skills	Standards
Call the Doctor	P: 15 min.	C, L	History	Compare and contrast past and present community helpers	NCHS 1
	A: 10 min.		Theatre	Act by assuming roles	MENC T-2
			Language Arts	Rhyming	NCTE 3
			Economics	Name community helpers	NCEE, 13
			Technology	Use technology to promote creativity	ISTE 3
A Penny a Pie	P: 25 min.	C, L	History	Compare and contrast past and present community helpers	NCHS 1
	A: 15 min.		Language Arts	Rhyming	NCTE 3
			Economics	Understand money; name community helpers	NCEE 11, 13
			Science	Properties of objects-colors	NAS-B
			Math	Count & sort objects; organize & graph data; problem solving	NCTM 1, 2, 5, 6

P: Approximate Preparation Time   **A:** Approximate Activity Time   **C:** Classroom Activity
H: Home Activity   **L:** Library Activity

8

Call the Doctor

Children act out the parts of doctor, patient, and parent as they repeat "The Cat's Got the Measles" rhyme from *Here Comes Mother Goose*. Like other activities for *Here Comes Mother Goose*, this one will help children compare occupations of the past and present.

Supplies:

- ◆ One copy of cat mask reproducible
- ◆ Toy doctor kit
- ◆ One wooden paint stirrer
- ◆ Hot glue gun and hot glue
- ◆ Crayons
- ◆ Optional: Two toy telephones

Preparation:

- ◆ Color the cat mask, adding red spots for measles. Cut out and laminate.
- ◆ Glue the wooden paint stirrer to the back of the mask.

Discussion:

(Ask after completing the activity.)

In the past a doctor would often come to a patient's house to take care of the patient. This was known as a house call.

> Do doctors still make house calls?

> Where do you go to see a doctor?

Discuss how in the past almost all doctors were men and nurses were women. Now women and men are doctors and nurses.

> How many of you have a man doctor?

> How many of you have a woman doctor?

> When you visit the doctor's office, how can you tell the doctor from the nurse?

> How are their jobs the same?

> How are they different?

Activity:

1. Choose one child to be the doctor, one to be the cat patient, and one to be the parent who calls the doctor.

2. Hand out props. (If you are not using toy telephones, show the children how to pretend they are talking on the phone.)

3. Show the children the illustrations on page 52 of the book as you all recite the first half of the rhyme.

4. The child who is the parent will say, "I'll call the doctor!"

5. Have the group recite the second half of the rhyme.

6. After the entire rhyme has been chanted, the parent pretends to call the doctor.

7. After answering the phone, the doctor will say, "I'll be right there!" The doctor will use the props from the doctor kit to pretend to take care of the sick cat, who will, of course, feel better.

8. When a girl is chosen to be the doctor, change the "he" in the last line of the rhyme to "she."

9. Play until everyone has had a turn.

Tech Tie-In:

◆ www.librarysupport.net/mothergoosesociety/

Visit the home page of the Mother Goose Society to print out Mother Goose rhymes, complete with recipes for children to take home. Be sure to check the Prop Box link for other fun activities. (At the time of this publication, the site included a link to send a free e-mail card celebrating Mother Goose Day, May 1st.)

◆ Add music to activities by selecting from the many musical versions of Mother Goose rhymes. Kimbo has several, including a Parent's Choice Award Winner, *Nursery Rhyme Time*. This is available as a cassette or CD. Both include a teacher's guide.

Nursery Rhyme Time. Georgiana Stewart, 2000. Includes guide with lyrics/activities. Kimbo Educational. (P.O. Box 477, Long Branch, NJ 07740)

Cat Mask

11

A Penny a Pie

It's hard to decide what pie is your favorite when there are so many to choose from. After reciting *Simple Simon*, children will enjoy choosing a pie from the flavors available, then making a class graph to see which pie is the group favorite.

Supplies:

◆ Four copies of pie reproducible

◆ Crayons

◆ Dry erase board or laminated white poster board

◆ Black dry erase marker

◆ Masking tape

◆ One penny for each child

◆ Four small disposable cups

Preparation:

◆ Color the pans on one page of the pie reproducible blue, one page yellow, one page orange, and one page red. Color all the crusts brown.

◆ Turn the dry erase board so the shortest sides are at the top and bottom. Draw one horizontal line across the top and one across the bottom, 4–5 inches from the edge. Divide the rest of the board into four equal vertical columns. In the space at the top of the board, write "What is your favorite pie?"

◆ At the bottom of the board, tape a red pie under the first column. Write "Cherry" in the space above the pie. Follow this step for the remaining columns: Lemon (yellow); Pumpkin (orange); and Blueberry (blue).

◆ Place a small paper cup underneath each pie. Place a small piece of masking tape on the back of each pie.

Discussion:

(Ask after reading the rhyme on page 28 and before completing the activity.)

Long ago when this nursery rhyme was written, someone who baked and sold pies may have been called a pieman.

Today what do we call someone who bakes pies? (baker)

12

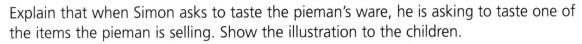

Explain that when Simon asks to taste the pieman's ware, he is asking to taste one of the items the pieman is selling. Show the illustration to the children.

> How is the pieman delivering his pies?
> Is this how pies are delivered today?
> Why can't Simon buy a pie from the pieman?
> How does Simon finally get a pie?

(Ask after completing the activity.)

As a group, count the number of pies in the first column. Write the number at the top of the column.

> How many pennies should we have in the cup?

Count the pennies. Repeat for each column.

> Which flavor of pie is the favorite?
> How many pies are in that column?
> Which is the least favorite?
> How many pies are in that column?

Compare other columns.

Activity:

1. Tell the children that, unlike Simon, they will each have a penny to buy a pie from you.

2. Show them the different flavors of pies and reinforce the flavor and color: "We have lemon pies. The lemon pies are yellow."

3. Purchase the first pie for yourself. Show the children how you pay for the pie and place it in one of the columns. Remove your pie and encourage the children to select their favorites.

4. Give each child a penny. Have each one take a turn by placing a penny in the cup under his/her favorite pie.

5. After you hand out the selected pie, help each child place his/her pie in the correct place on the class graph. Complete the discussion.

Challenge:

Do this challenge activity to help children with spatial relationships. After completing the activity, reduce the space between the pies in the column containing the most pies. Space them closely so that this is no longer the tallest column. Ask the children which column has the most pies. Count the pies again so the children begin to understand that the number of pies did not change, even though their placement in the column changed.

Pie Reproducible

14

In the Tall, Tall Grass
by Denise Fleming

JUV
591
F59i

Fleming, Denise, *In the Tall, Tall Grass.*
H. Holt, 1991, 32 pp., 0-8050-1635-X

Look at everything from a caterpillar's point of view as you see all of the animals hiding in the tall grass. The bold handmade paper illustrations convey excitement and are easily seen from a distance. Combined with rhyming words that mimic the movements and sounds of common animals, this book is a natural for storytime.

◆ Skills Table ◆

Activity	Time	Location	Subjects	Skills	Standards
Indoor Nature Walk	P: none A: 10 min.	C, H, L	Language Arts Geography Math	Read for information and pleasure Spatial perspective (left and right) Repeat patterns of sounds	NCTE 1 NGS 1 NCTM 2
A Closer Look	P: 10 min. A: 15 min.	C, H, L	Language Arts Science Technology	Understand print conveys meaning Develop scientific inquiry skills; observe properties of objects Compare & evaluate print and electronic media	NCTE 3 NAS-A, B ISTE 5

P: Approximate Preparation Time   **A:** Approximate Activity Time   **C:** Classroom Activity
H: Home Activity   **L:** Library Activity

In the Tall, Tall Grass by Denise Fleming

Indoor Nature Walk

During this indoor adventure, children can chant and imagine all the things they might see on a walk through the tall grass.

Supplies:

◆ Dry erase board

Preparation:

◆ None

Activity:

(Complete after reading the book to the children.)

1. Show the illustrations to the children as you discuss the animals and insects that appeared in the book.

2. As the children name each one, write it on the board and draw a simple sketch of the insect or animal next to the word.

3. Be sure to put the snake at the bottom of the list so it is the last animal of the game.

    Note: You may wish to tell the children that the snake in the book is a nonpoisonous grass snake, but they need to be very careful in the wild where it is difficult to tell the difference between poisonous and nonpoisonous snakes.

4. Tell the children they are going on a pretend walk in the tall grass where they will see each of the animals or insects written on the board.

5. Show them how to make the swishing grass sound by placing their palms together and sliding their hands back and forth. They should make the swishing grass sound throughout the walk.

6. When the children turn their heads left and right, turn yours to match their motion.

7. Recite one line at a time. Have the children repeat the line.

8. As you say the name of each animal, point to the word on the dry erase board.

16

We're Going on a Nature Walk

Repeat stanzas three and four for each animal on the list except the snake.

1. We're going on a nature walk,
   To see what we can see.
   We're walking through the tall grass,
   As happy as can be.

2. We look to the left, *(look to the children's left)*
   We look to the right, *(look to the children's right)*
   What we see
   Is quite a sight.

3. Straight ahead,
   In front of me, *(look to the front)*
   I see a <u>*(insert name of animal or insect)*</u>
   Looking at me.

4. He looks to the left, *(look to the children's left)*
   He looks to the right, *(look to the children's right)*
   And then he scurries
   Out of sight!

Use these verses for the snake ending:

3. Straight ahead,
   In front of me, *(look to the front)*
   I see a snake
   Looking at me.

4. I look to the left,
   I look to the right,
   And then I scurry
   Out of sight!

5. Back through the tall grass, *(rub hands together faster and faster)*
   Running all the way,
   Then back inside, *(pretend to open door and slam door)*
   That's where I'm going to play! *(point to yourself)*
   (Pause)
   At least today!

17

A Closer Look

This tactile activity challenges children to take a closer look. Let children take turns finding the unusual things hiding in the grass.

Supplies:

◆ Large clear plastic bowl

◆ One package of green Easter grass

◆ Dry erase board and marker

◆ Variety of small to medium-sized objects: button, colored jumbo paper clip, wooden craft stick, crayon, cotton ball, sandpaper, balloon, clothespin, ribbon, spoon. *(Make sure some of the items are green.)*

Preparation:

◆ Put the grass in the large clear bowl.

Discussion:

(Ask after reading the book to the children.)

Show the book illustrations to the children as you ask the questions.

Is it easier to see the green snake in the grass or the brightly colored hummingbird?

Would it be easier for you or for the caterpillar to see the tiny ants in the grass? Why?

Activity:

1. Select items to hide in the bowl. For younger children, hide bigger objects that are not easily camouflaged.

2. As the children watch, select an item and add it to the bowl. Print the name of that item on the dry erase board, then draw a simple picture next to the word to illustrate it.

3. Ask all the children to help you check off each item as it is found by saying the name of the item. Items do not need to be found in order.

4. Have each child take an object from the bowl. Remind them to use their senses of touch and sight to take *only one object*. Collect each item from the children as they find it.

Variation:

◆ For a more difficult version, have children find items in the same order they are listed, or have children wear a blindfold and use only their sense of touch to find an item on the list.

Tech Tie-In:

◆ Watch this video of *In the Tall, Tall Grass*. Compare the video to the book.

In the Tall, Tall Grass. 1992. 6 minutes. Spoken Arts.
(P.O. Box 100, New Rochelle, NY 10802)

Little Cloud
by Eric Carle

Carle, Eric, *Little Cloud*. Philomel, 1996, 26 pp., 0-399-23034-5

In this simple story, Little Cloud spends his day making interesting shapes in the sky. Finally, he joins the other clouds as they group together to do what clouds do best…rain. The bold collage and paint illustrations will appeal to young children and are perfect for sharing at storytime.

◆ Skills Table ◆

Activity	Time	Location	Subjects	Skills	Standards
Rain Parade	P: none	C, L	Science	Observe changes in weather; become aware of water cycle	NAS-D
	A: 10 min.		Language Arts	Rhyming; appreciate textual features	NCTE 3
			Dance	Copy movements; use dance to communicate	MENC D-1, D-3
			Music	Sing in groups	MENC M-1
			Technology	Use technology to collect information	ISTE 5
My Pet Cloud	P: 20 min.	C, H, L	Art	Understand & apply media	MENC A-1
	A: 10 min.		Language Arts	Appreciate textual features-rhyming	NCTE 3

P: Approximate Preparation Time **A:** Approximate Activity Time **C:** Classroom Activity
H: Home Activity **L:** Library Activity

Rain Parade

Help children understand the water cycle as they pretend to be water drops that evaporate into the sky to form a cloud. When the cloud becomes so heavy, watch out for the rain!

Supplies:

◆ Dry erase board and markers

Preparation:

◆ None

Discussion:

(Read the book to the children before drawing this example.)

Tell the children that clouds are made up of tiny water drops. *(Draw a group of water drops at the top of the board to form a faint cloud.)*

The water drops come from the oceans and rivers. *(Draw a squiggle and a circle below the cloud.)*

When the sun shines on the oceans and rivers, some of the water evaporates or goes into the air. *(Draw a sun.)*

The drops are so tiny that you can't see them until there are enough to make a cloud. *(Add more drops to the cloud.)*

When a cloud has lots of water drops, it gets heavy. That's what makes rain. *(Draw rain drops.)* The water goes back into the oceans and rivers.

Activity:

1. Teach the children the "Rain Parade" song. You will be the sun shining on the sea. The children will be water drops from the sea. They will evaporate, change from water drops to a cloud, and finally raindrops.

2. As you sing the first verse, link hands to form a winding line with everyone facing the same direction. Lead the children around the room. At the end of the song, all of the children will be sitting on the floor in their original locations.

Rain Parade

(Sing to the tune of "London Bridge")

Repeat the first verse until all children are holding hands.

1. The sun shone on the deep blue sea,
   Deep blue sea, deep blue sea,
   It called to the water drops
   Play with me, play with me-ee.

Form a circle.

2. Water drops up in the sky,
   In the sky, in the sky,
   Make a clo-oud floating by,
   Floating by-y.

Stop walking and drop hands. As you sing the third verse, prompt one child at a time to quietly sit down. Continue to sing the third verse until all children are seated.

3. Heavy, heavy in the sky,
   In the sky, in the sky,
   Raindrops falling by and by,
   Raindrops falling.

Sing the fourth verse as the children stand and return to their seats.

4. Back to the rivers,
   And the sea, and the sea, and the sea,
   Back to the flowers and the trees,
   Raindrops falling.

Tech Tie-In:

http://www.reachoutmichigan.org/funexperiments/quick/raincloud.html

Connect with this Web site to make a cloud that really rains. All you need is a sponge, water, and bowl. This site from Southeastern Michigan Math-Science Learning Coalition and Reach Out Michigan contains a searchable database of science lessons by subject and grade level. There is even a special list of quick and easy activities.

My Pet Cloud

Children can design their own pet cloud bookmark with features to make the cloud their own special pet.

Supplies:

◆ One My Pet Cloud reproducible for each child plus two extras

◆ Washable markers or colored pencils

◆ Hole punch

◆ One 12" length of yarn for each child plus two extras

Preparation:

◆ Cut out bookmarks. Punch out the small circle on each cloud and thread the yarn through the hole. Tie a knot close to the bookmark.

◆ Make two sample bookmarks. Add animal features, color, and print the name of each animal in the blank.

Discussion:

(Ask after reading the book to the children.)

Show one of the cloud illustrations from the book.

What does this cloud look like? *(Answers will vary.)*

Does everyone see the same thing when they look at clouds?

What are some of the animals you have seen when you looked at clouds?

Activity:

1. Show the children your sample pet cloud bookmarks. Read the rhyme to the children and tell them they will get to make their own pet cloud.

2. Point out the features you added to your clouds to make them look more like animals. Encourage children to be creative and turn their cloud into any kind of animal they want.

3. After they finish turning their cloud into an animal and coloring the bookmark, print the name of their animal in the blank.

4. Show children how to use the bookmark.

My Pet Cloud

I have a very special pet,
like one you've never met.
It doesn't bark or shed its hair;
it eats no more than air.

If I could put it on a leash,
I'd take it home to play,
Then let it go to soar up high and
be a _____ in the sky.

My Pet Cloud

I have a very special pet,
like one you've never met.
It doesn't bark or shed its hair;
it eats no more than air.

If I could put it on a leash,
I'd take it home to play,
Then let it go to soar up high and
be a _____ in the sky.

Mouse Count

by Ellen Stohl Walsh

JUV
W225mc

Walsh, Ellen Stohl, *Mouse Count*. Harcourt Brace, 1991, 32 pp., 0-15-256023-8

Although the size of this book is small, the simple text and bold collages make it a natural for storytime. The playfulness of the mice as they romp through the meadow is sure to bring a smile to the face of young listeners. It's easy to get them involved in the story as they count along with the greedy snake and predict what will happen next to the unfortunate mice.

◆ Skills Table ◆

Activity	Time	Location	Subjects	Skills	Standards
Rock 'n Roll	P: 20 min.	C, H, L	Math	Understand relationships among numbers	NCTM 1
	A: 20 min.		Language Arts	Story recall	NCTE 3
Snake Bite	P: 10 min.	L, C, H	Math	Understand patterns	NCTM 2
	A: 20 min.		Art	Use different media to communicate ideas	MENC A-1

P: Approximate Preparation Time **A:** Approximate Activity Time **C:** Classroom Activity
H: Home Activity **L:** Library Activity

Rock 'n Roll

Children can recreate the mouse escape as they rock the jar back and forth and do their own mouse count.

Supplies:

- ◆ One piece of gray, black or brown craft foam
- ◆ Ruler
- ◆ Hole Punch
- ◆ Scissors
- ◆ One 45" length of black yarn
- ◆ Black fine point permanent marker
- ◆ Construction paper, blue and red
- ◆ One clear plastic container
- ◆ Six unlined 3" x 5" index cards

Preparation:

- ◆ Cut ten egg-size mice from craft foam. Add features as shown above. Punch a hole for the tail at the dot mark.
- ◆ Cut ten 4½" mouse tails from black yarn. Thread the yarn through the hole and tie a knot close to the mouse body to make the mouse tail.
- ◆ Cut the index cards in half, crosswise. Number cards from zero to ten. Mark two cards with the number five.

Activity:

(Complete after reading the book to the children.)

1. Give each child a turn dropping a mouse into the jar while the group counts out loud.

2. Let children take turns tipping the jar to shake one group of mice onto the red paper. Leave some mice in the jar. Count the mice aloud and place the matching number card by the mice.

3. Repeat the step, shaking the remaining mice onto the blue paper.

4. Ask the children to add the two number cards together by counting all the mice. The answer should always be ten. Place the number ten card next to the mice after each count.

5. Repeat until the children have added several different number combinations.

Snake Bite

Children can design their own cereal snakes and share a snack in this enjoyable activity.

Supplies:

◆ One chenille stem for each child plus two extra

◆ One box of Kellogg's Froot Loops® cereal

◆ One 2½" paper baking cup for each child

◆ One aerosol can of green decorating icing

◆ One bottle round cake decorating candies in assorted colors

◆ Red acrylic yarn, cut in 1" pieces

◆ One ¼-cup measuring container

Preparation:

◆ Slightly bend one end of the chenille stem.

◆ Thread cereal onto the stem, designing at least two different patterns. Cover all but the last three inches of the stem.

◆ Thread two more matching cereal pieces for eyes. Slide them to the middle of the empty part of the chenille stem while you bend the end of the stem back and tuck it into the last piece of cereal in the pattern. This forms a loop for the head.

◆ Cut a 1" piece of yarn. Put one end of the yarn up into the loop of the head so that it hangs down like a tongue.

◆ Pinch the chenille stem together around the end of the tongue to secure it.

◆ Spread the eyes apart so the holes in the cereal are facing the front, and slide them forward.

◆ Put a dot of green icing at the top of each eye, above the chenille stem.

◆ Pick two pieces of cake decorating candy for the pupils of the eyes, and stick them in the green icing.

◆ Measure out ¼ cup of cereal in a paper baking cup for each child.

Discussion:

(Ask after reading the book and before the activity.)

Show the children the snake illustrations from the book.

What color are the snake's stripes?

Point out the snake's green-yellow stripe pattern. This snake's stripes are in pairs of green and yellow. These are called patterns.

Does the snake have any other colors of stripes?

Does the snake have any other patterns?

Point to an illustration that shows just the head of the snake. This snake has a pattern of two stripes.

Can you guess what pattern comes next on the part of the snake you can't see?

(Ask after completing the activity.)

How many pieces of cereal did you use to make your snake?

What color of stripes does your snake have?

How many stripes are in your pattern?

How many different patterns does your snake have?

Activity:

1. Show the children your sample snake and tell them they are going to design their own.

2. Encourage them to create their own pattern.

3. If they run out of some of the colors they need to complete their pattern, help them create a second pattern for their snake.

4. Assist them in making the head of the snake.

5. Add the icing to the each child's cereal eyes and place the candy pupils on the icing.

6. Finish the discussion.

7. Let the children snack on extra cereal from their cups while they share information about their snakes.

Quack and Count
by Keith Baker

JUV 513.2 B167q (handwritten)

Baker, Keith, *Quack and Count*. Harcourt Brace, 1999, 20 pp., 0-15-292858-8

Children will learn all the different ways to count to seven by following seven ducklings through their busy day. This book is a natural for teaching children to add, since the seven ducklings regroup themselves in many ways. The colorful collage illustrations and rhyming text make this a good read-aloud for storytime.

◆ Skills Table ◆

Activity	Time	Location	Subjects	Skills	Standards
Hide and Seek	P: 10 min. A: 15 min.	C, H, L	Science Art Language Arts	Ask questions about objects; use senses Select subject matter Story recall	NAS-A MENC A-3 NCTE 1
Let's Go For a Swim	P: none A: 10 min.	L, C, H	Math Music Theatre	Theatre subtraction Sing in groups Act by assuming roles	NCTM 1 MENC M-1 MENC T-2

P: Approximate Preparation Time   **A:** Approximate Activity Time   **C:** Classroom Activity
H: Home Activity   **L:** Library Activity

Hide and Seek

What do the ducks see when they put their heads under water? Children will love finding out when they make their own underwater scene.

Supplies:

- ◆ One container of multicolor glitter
- ◆ Three large bottles of blue hair gel
- ◆ One sandwich-size plastic zipper bag for each child
- ◆ Copy paper
- ◆ Washable markers or crayons

Preparation:

Prepare underwater bags by squeezing blue hair gel into the plastic zipper bags. Fill the bags approximately half full. Shake a small amount of glitter in each bag and zip securely, removing as much air from the bags as possible.

Discussion:

(Ask after reading the book but before doing the activity.)

Show some of the animal illustrations from the book.

> What kinds of animals live in the water in a pond?
>
> Do some of the animals stay in the water all of the time? Why?
>
> Would it be easier for a duck to see the animals that live under the water or for you to see those animals? Why?
>
> What would a duck need to do to see the animals near the bottom of a pond?

(Ask after children have completed the activity.)

> What do you think the sparkly water is made from?
>
> How does it feel when you push the sparkly water around with your fingers?

Activity:

1. Have each child draw several animals that a duck might see under the water.

2. After the pictures are drawn, give each child a bag containing the hair gel and glitter mixture.

3. Show children how to place their bag over the underwater scene and push the sparkly waves around until they can see all the animals hiding under the water.

4. Complete the discussion section as children look at their underwater scenes.

30

Let's Go For a Swim

Sing this counting song as a fingerplay or let seven children at a time act out the words as they pretend to be happy little ducks playing in the summer sun.

Supplies:

◆ None

Preparation:

◆ None

Activity:

1. Teach the children the "Seven Ducks" song, then choose seven children at a time to act out the words. *(If less than seven children are available to act out the song, change the first verse to reflect the number of players.)*

2. As each verse is sung, one child will leave the group of ducks chasing bugs to join the ducks swimming. When the last verse is sung, all seven children will be pretending to swim, and none will be chasing bugs.

Seven Ducks

(Sing to the tune of "London Bridge")

Seven ducks were having fun,
Chasing bugs, in the sun.
One was hot, but six were not,
One went swimming!

Six ducks were having fun,
Chasing bugs, in the sun.
One was hot, but five were not,
One went swimming!

Five ducks were having fun,
Chasing bugs, in the sun.
One was hot, but four were not,
One went swimming!

Four ducks were having fun,
Chasing bugs, in the sun.
One was hot, but three were not,
One went swimming!

Three ducks were having fun,
Chasing bugs, in the sun.
One was hot,
But two were not,
One went swimming!

Two ducks were having fun,
Chasing bugs, in the sun.
One was hot,
But one was not,
One went swimming!

One duck was having fun,
Chasing bugs, in the sun.
He was hot,
The rest were not,
They *all* went swimming!

No ducks were having fun,
Chasing bugs, in the sun.
But seven ducks were having fun,
Swimming in the river!

Variation:

Use gestures as indicated below to act out the song. The number of fingers held up will change with each verse to reflect the number of ducks.

Seven ducks were having fun	*(Hold up seven fingers)*
Chasing bugs, in the sun.	*(Open and shut the right hand in a quacking motion)*
One was hot,	*(Fan yourself, then hold up one finger)*
But six were not,	*(Hold up six fingers and shake head "no")*
One went swimming!	*(Hold up one finger. Put hands together in a diving motion.)*

Snowy Day

JUV
K25s
C.19

by Ezra Jack Keats

Keats, Ezra Jack, *The Snowy Day*. Viking Press, 1962, 32 pp., 0-670-65400-0

When Peter wakes up and sees all the snow that has fallen during the night, he is quick to go outside and play. The expressive collage illustrations of this Caldecott Medal winner show a young child experiencing the simple pleasures of a snowy day in his neighborhood.

Children familiar with snow will identify with Peter's adventures, while those who have never experienced snow will have the perfect introduction.

◆ Skills Table ◆

Activity	Time	Location	Subjects	Skills	Standards
Snowball Fun	P: 15 min.	L, C	Math	Count; compare numbers; estimation	NCTM 1
	A: 10–15 min.		Language Arts	Rhyming; verbalization	NCTE 3, 4
			Technology	Compare & evaluate print and electronic media	ISTE 5
			Health	Dressing for weather conditions	AAHE 3

P: Approximate Preparation Time   **A:** Approximate Activity Time   **C:** Classroom Activity
H: Home Activity   **L:** Library Activity

Snowball Fun

Children can practice counting and estimating as they say the chant and decide how many snowballs they'll need for a snowball fight.

Supplies:

- One bag of cotton balls
- Paper and pencil
- One piece of felt
- One copy of Snowball Fun reproducible
- One white chenille stem, bent into a triangle shape
- Scissors
- Glue stick
- Flannel board
- Markers or crayons

Preparation:

- Color the reproducible, then laminate and cut out each figure.
- Cut and glue three small squares of felt to the back of each figure.
- Bend the chenille stem into a triangle.

Activity:

(Complete after reading the book to the children.)

1. Put the pictures of the boys across from each other on the flannel board. Tell the children the boys want to have a snowball fight. What are they missing? Snowballs, of course.

2. Show the children the picture in *Snowy Day* where the boys are having a snowball fight. Talk about how children often make stacks of snowballs so they will have lots of snowballs ready to throw. The snowballs are often stacked in a shape like the triangle.

3. Put the triangle chenille stem on the flannel board between the boys. Tell the children they are going to make a stack of snowballs for the snowball fight. Demonstrate stacking the snowballs by gently pressing a cotton ball inside the triangle shape.

4. Ask the children how many snowballs will fit inside this triangle. *(Write down three or four of the answers.)*

5. Teach the children the rhyme, counting to ten and holding up one finger for each number.

6. Give each child a snowball. Choose one child at a time to gently place a snowball inside the triangle as the group says the rhyme. Continue counting until all snowballs are on the flannel board.

7. If there are extra snowballs, add them to the flannel board as snowballs whizzing through the air or lying on the ground. If the triangle is not full, give children more snowballs for the triangle.

8. How many snowballs did it take to fill up the triangle? *(Write down the actual number of snowballs.)*

9. Was that more or less than what we thought? *(Compare the actual amount to each estimate.)*

Snowball Fun

Stack those snowballs,
Stack them high.
Stack them 'till they reach the sky.
How many snowballs can you stack?
1   2   3   4   5   *(Continue counting until all the snowballs are on the board.)*

Tech Tie-In:

◆ Children can compare the book and video when they watch *The Snowy Day*. Which do the children like best?

Watch and compare the other Ezra Jack Keats videos in this collection:

Ezra Jack Keats Video Library: The Snowy Day, Whistle for Willie, Peter's Chair, A Letter to Amy, Pet Show, and The Trip. 1996. 37 min. Weston Woods. (265 Post Road West, Westport, CT 06880)

◆ Shop online for mittens, hats, coats, and other clothing to wear for the snowball fight.

Snowball Fun Boys

Trucks, Trucks, Trucks JUV 3622t
by Peter Sis

Sis, Peter, *Trucks, Trucks, Trucks*. Greenwillow Books, 1999, 24 pp., 0-688-16276-2

A little boy picks up the trucks in his room by pretending to drive them. He makes the job look like so much fun kids will be anxious to use their own trucks to pick up their rooms. The book is just the right size for small hands to carry, and the big, simple pictures and minimal text make it easy to notice the important details of each kind of truck.

◆ Skills Table ◆

Activity	Time	Location	Subjects	Skills	Standards
Construction Ahead	P: 10 min. A: 10 min.	C, L	Health Music Dance Technology	Compare safe and risky behaviors Sing in groups Locomotor movements Collect information	AAHE 3 MENC- M1 MENC- D1 ISTE 5
My Trucks	P: none A: 5 min.	C, H, L	Dance Language Arts	Repeat large and small motor movements Communicate effectively by speaking	MENC- D1 NCTE 4

P: Approximate Preparation Time   **A:** Approximate Activity Time   **C:** Classroom Activity
H: Home Activity   **L:** Library Activity

Trucks, Trucks, Trucks by Peter Sis

Construction Ahead

Practice obeying traffic signs while singing a song in this fun group activity. The song is a perfect way to line up children at the close of storytime.

Supplies:

- ◆ Construction paper: red and orange
- ◆ Two wooden paint stirring sticks
- ◆ Hot glue gun and glue
- ◆ Wide-point black marker
- ◆ Glue stick
- ◆ Scissors
- ◆ Ruler

Preparation:

- ◆ Cut two orange and two red octagon signs from construction paper. Make each sign as large as possible.
- ◆ With the black marker, print SLOW on the orange signs and STOP on the red.
- ◆ Create two sets of signs by placing one red STOP and one orange SLOW sign back-to-back. With hot glue, sandwich a paint stirrer between the signs at the base to serve as a handle. Use a glue stick to glue the edges of the signs together. Repeat to make the second sign set.

Activity:

1. Choose two children as construction workers to hold the signs. Have them stand at opposite ends of the room, facing each other.

2. Divide the rest of the class into two groups. (The groups do *not* need to have equal numbers of children.) Each group will line up behind one of the construction workers.

3. Have one construction worker turn his/her sign so the STOP side faces the group behind him/her. The other will turn his/her sign so the SLOW side faces the group behind him/her.

4. Explain that during road construction, only one lane is open to traffic. The groups will take turns "driving" in opposite directions in the lane.

5. Begin with the group facing the STOP sign. They will sing the first stanza of the song. No one should be driving.

6. Lead the group with the SLOW sign facing them in singing the second stanza of the song as you slowly "drive" to the opposite end of the room and loop around to where you began.

7. As soon as the last person in the group is past the SLOW sign, the construction worker will turn his/her sign to the STOP side.

8. The other construction worker flips his/her sign.

9. Repeat steps 5 through 7. Play the game as many times as desired.

When the Sign Says Slow
(Sing to the tune of "When the Saints Go Marching In")

Oh when the sign,
Oh when the sign,
Oh when the si-gn says to STOP,
You'd better wait for the traffic,
When the si-gn says to STOP.

Oh when the sign,
Oh when the sign,
Oh when the si-gn says go SLOW,
You'd better drive oh so slowly,
When the si-gn says go SLOW.

Tech Tie-In:

◆ This award-winning video shows the road construction process from start to finish:

> *Road Construction Ahead.* 1991. 30 minutes. Fred Levine Productions.
> (64 Main St., Suite 26, Montpelier, VT 05602)

◆ With a digital camera, photograph the safety signs in the vicinity of the school. Create a computer page of the photographs that can be printed out for children to take home. Encourage children to walk around the school with family members to locate all these important safety signs.

My Trucks

Follow up the story *Trucks, Trucks, Trucks* by Peter Sis with this fingerplay. A variation turns the rhyme into a large motor skill activity that will have the children pretending to be dump trucks, bulldozers, and cranes.

Supplies:

◆ None

Preparation:

◆ None

Discussion:

(Ask after reading the book to the children.)

Show the truck illustrations from the book, one at a time.

> What is this truck's job?
>
> How can you tell?

Continue asking these questions about other types of trucks in the book.

Show the illustrations of the little boy's room at the beginning of the book and the illustration of the street at the end of the book.

> Which picture has more trucks?
>
> What kinds of trucks are outside that the little boy doesn't have in his room?

Activity:

◆ Teach the fingerplay to the children.

40

My Trucks

The dump truck dumps,

(Place hands on top of each other in front of your chest. Lift top hand in a dumping motion.)

The bulldozer pushes,

(Both hands make fists and starting at chest, push away from your body)

And the big tall crane lifts high.

(Place one fist on top of other in front of chest. Lift top arm above head.)

But there's one thing

(Hold up one finger.)

That they all need…

It's me to sit inside!

(Point to yourself.)

Variation:

This adaptation of the fingerplay can be used as a large motor skill activity. Have children kneel down with their bottom resting on their feet.

My Trucks

The dump truck dumps,

(Bend head to knees and then return to upright position.)

The bulldozer pushes,

(Make fists. Push hands along the floor away from the body.)

And the big tall crane lifts high.

(Raise arms above head and stand up.)

But there's one thing

(Hold up one finger.)

That they all need…

It's me to sit inside!

(Point to yourself.)

What the Sun Sees,
What the Moon Sees

JUV
T124wh

by Nancy Tafuri

**Tafuri, Nancy, *What the Sun Sees, What the Moon Sees*.
Greenwillow Books, 1997, 32 pp., 0-688-14494-2**

This unusual book combines two stories in one. Read halfway through to find out what the sun sees, then turn the book around and see how different things look when the sun goes down and the moon comes up. The peaceful night pictures and comparisons between night and day will prove reassuring to those children fearful of the dark.

◆ Skills Table ◆

Activity	Time	Location	Subjects	Skills	Standards
My Blanket	P: none A: 3 min.	C, H, L	Language Arts Science	Repeat rhymes; vocabulary Ask questions about events in the environment	NCTE 3, 4 NAS- A
Like Night and Day	P: 15 min. A: 15 min.	C, H, L	Language Arts Geography	Read to acquire new information; Speak to exchange information Characteristics of places	NCTE 1, 12 NGS 4

P: Approximate Preparation Time   **A:** Approximate Activity Time   **C:** Classroom Activity
H: Home Activity   **L:** Library Activity

My Blanket

This fingerplay activity introduces *What the Sun Sees, What the Moon Sees*. Children can compare daytime activities to nighttime activities.

Supplies:

◆ None

Preparation:

◆ None

Discussion:

What are some things you do during the day?

What are some things you do during the night?

What things can only be done during the day? Why?

What things can only be done at night? Why?

Activity:

(Complete before reading the book to the children.)

Teach the children the fingerplay, then let them share the things they do during the day and things they do during the night. Can they think of people who work during the night and sleep during the day?

My Blanket

When the sun comes up each day,	*(Hands above head to form a circle.)*
I throw off my blanket .	*(Cross arms, then open wide.)*
Then run and play.	*(Move arms back and forth like running.)*
When the sun has gone away,	*(Hands above head to form a circle, then lower hands.)*
The moon shines down	*(Same motion as sun above head.)*
And lights the way	
To my bed where I will creep,	*(Pantomime taking small steps by moving hands.)*
Wrap up in my blanket	*(Cross arms and hug yourself.)*
And go to sleep.	*(Put palms together at side of face; lay head on hands.)*

What the Sun Sees, What the Moon Sees by Nancy Tafuri

Like Night and Day

This dual-purpose mask will let children pretend to be the moon and the sun. What do the sun and moon see? Peek out of the mask and find out.

Supplies:

◆ One Sun and Moon reproducible

◆ Scissors

◆ Clear adhesive tape

◆ Glue stick

◆ Yellow crayon

Preparation:

◆ Cut out the sun/moon picture. Glue it to the center of the paper plate.

◆ Cut through the rim of the paper plate to the bottom tip of the moon. Then cut along the crescent silhouette dividing the sun and moon.

◆ To create "hinges" for the sun and moon to swing on, measure and mark a one-inch hinge on the mid-right side of the moon. Do the same on the sun side.

◆ Cut around the perimeter of the sun and moon, but *do not cut these hinges*. When you have completed cutting around the perimeter, the moon and sun should swing open to the left and right.

◆ Tape the cut section of the rim back together on the back of the plate.

◆ Color the sun face yellow. Color yellow rays in the rim of the sun side of the plate. Leave the moon uncolored.

◆ On the back of the plate, lightly pencil a sun on the back of the moon and a moon on the back of the sun.

Activity:

(Complete after reading the book to the children.)

1. Show the children several pictures from the book. Compare the day and night pictures.

2. Hold the plate to your face like a mask.

3. Reading the pencil cues on the back on the plate, push open the side marked "sun."

4. As the children look at the sun, say, "Peek-a-Boo. The sun sees children listening to a story."

5. Close the mask and push open the other side so that the moon is visible to the children. Say, "Peek-a-Boo. The moon sees children sleeping."

6. Continue the game by holding up the mask and naming one thing from the book that the moon saw.

7. Have a child peek out of the mask and name the corresponding thing that the sun saw.

8. Encourage children to speak in complete sentences.

9. Play until all of the night and day scenes in the book have been described and every child has a turn holding the mask.

Variations:

◆ For a more difficult version, have one child hold the mask and name something not listed in the book that the sun would see. Another child will then take the mask and name the contrasting thing the moon would see.

◆ For younger children, have a child name something the sun might see, while you name the contrasting thing the moon might see.

Classroom Collaboration:

◆ Create a sun and moon kit for each child to take back to the classroom where their teachers can help them create their own masks.

◆ Encourage the children to take home the masks and discover with their families what the sun sees and what the moon sees.

Sun and Moon

Who Hoots?
by Katie Davis

JUV
D26198w

Davis, Katie, *Who Hoots?* Harcourt, 2000, 36 pp., 0-15-202312-7

This book, like Davis' earlier book *Who Hops?*, will have children roaring with laughter. Who says owls don't hoot? While *Who Hops?* compared animal movements, *Who Hoots?* compares animal sounds.

The fun comes from the children correcting all of the mistakes the book makes when it forgets that owls hoot, bees buzz, mice squeak, lions roar, and ducks quack. Children, of course, can make all of those sounds and will!

◆ Skills Table ◆

Activity	Time	Location	Subjects	Skills	Standards
What's Up?	P: 40 min.	C, H, L	Math	Sort by color, shape and size; spatial reasoning; symmetry; problem solving	NCTM 3, 6
	A: 15 min.		Science	Scientific inquiry skills; describe properties of objects	NAS- A, B
Who are You?	P: none	C, L	Language Arts	Rhyming words; differentiate between sounds	NCTE 3
	A: 10 min.		Science	Compare characteristics of various animals	NAS- C
			Health	Listening skills	AAHE 5
			Technology	Use technology to collect information	ISTE 5

P: Approximate Preparation Time   **A:** Approximate Activity Time   **C:** Classroom Activity
H: Home Activity   **L:** Library Activity

What's Up?

Children will use visual discrimination as they place their triangle or circle on the owl. What makes this puzzling owl stay stuck to the dry erase board? Experimentation with common household items will lead children to make discoveries about properties of objects and materials.

Supplies:

◆ Craft foam: one each of brown, yellow, orange, blue, green, red, and black

◆ One copy of owl pattern

◆ Dry erase board large enough for owl reproducible

◆ Black ball point pen

◆ Scissors

◆ One sponge

◆ One small shallow bowl

◆ One disposable plastic plate

◆ One 2" square of each: construction paper, waxed paper, aluminum foil, and medium grit sandpaper

Preparation:

◆ Transfer the pattern of the owl to brown craft foam and cut out.

◆ Trace the small circles and triangles onto the body so the craft foam owl matches the pattern, except for the eyes. To duplicate the eyes, transfer the largest circles first, then the middle, and finally the small circles.

◆ Cut out the triangle and circle shapes from craft foam in colors noted on the owl pattern reproducible.

◆ Fill the small bowl with about two inches of water. Wet the sponge and place it on the plate.

◆ Place all the materials near the board.

Discussion:

(Ask after reading the book to the children.)

Ask the children which animal hoots. Then tell them they will get to make a special owl. As they watch, wipe the wet sponge across the back of the brown owl body and gently press it to the dry erase board.

> What do you think was on the sponge that made the owl stick to the dry erase board?

The owl is made from a special kind of foam called craft foam.

> Have you ever seen bath toy blocks and shapes made from craft foam?
> What happens when the wet craft foam is pressed to the side of the bathtub?
> What makes the bath toys stick to the side of the bathtub?

Show the children the squares of construction paper, wax paper, foil, and sandpaper.

> Which of these do you think will stick to the board when they are wet?

One at a time, wipe the sponge across each item and try sticking each to the board. *(All of the items except the rough sand paper should stick, if wet enough.)*

> What do all of the things that stuck to the dry erase board have in common? *(all flat and smooth)*
> What happens if you turn the sandpaper over and wet the smooth side before sticking it to the board? *(It will stick.)*

Activity:

1. Wet the back of a large, medium and small circle. Stick them above the owl on the dry erase board.

2. Point to each one and ask the children to describe the size, color, and shape of each circle.

3. Repeat with the triangles.

4. Hand out all of the shapes, saying the color and shape as the child receives it. For example, "You have a small, black circle."

5. Give each child a turn at placing his/her shape in a matching spot on the owl.

6. Help them wipe each piece of craft foam with the sponge before pressing it *gently* to the appropriate spot on the owl. (To assemble the eyes, start with the large circle, then medium and small.)

7. Let children practice hooting after the puzzling owl is finished.

8. If time permits, leave the owl on the board. Eventually the water will evaporate and the owl will fall off.

49

Owl Pattern

Cut out the following: Yellow: two large triangles, three large circles, three medium triangles; Orange: two medium triangles, seven small triangles, three medium circles; Blue: two medium triangles; Green: two medium triangles; Black: three small circles.

Who Are You?

Use this rhyming game to help children work on auditory discrimination skills while they have fun making animal sounds.

Supplies:

◆ None

Preparation:

◆ None

Activity:

(Complete after reading the book to the children.)

1. Teach children the "If You Could Be An Animal" rhyme. Recite using a cow as an example.

2. Give each child a turn to make an animal sound.

3. Have other children raise their hands to guess what animal the child was pretending to be.

4. If no one can guess the name of the animal, the child who made the animal sound will tell the group the name of the animal. Encourage children to repeat the rhyme with you.

If You Could Be an Animal

Group:	If you could be an animal, What would you say To all the other animals Each and every day?
Child:	Moo! Moo! Moo! *(substitute other animal sounds)*
Group:	That's what she (or he) would say To all the other animals Each and every day.
Child:	Who am I?

Tech Tie-In:

- http://www.wildsanctuary.com/safari.html
- Let children click on the Listen button next to the picture to hear the sounds of animals from around the world. Read the text to explain why the animal makes that sound.

Baby Duck and the Bad Eyeglasses
by Amy Hest

Hest, Amy, *Baby Duck and the Bad Eyeglasses*. Candlewick Press, 1996, 28 pp., 1-56402-680-9

Baby Duck does not like her new glasses. Not only does she not look like herself, but she's afraid to try any of the things she used to do for fear her glasses will fall off. Mr. and Mrs. Duck are unable to console her, but, as always, Grampa knows just what to do. Baby Duck finds that not only can she do all of the things she used to, she can do even more now that she can see clearly.

◆ Skills Table ◆

Activity	Time	Location	Subjects	Skills	Standards
Glasses for Fun	P: none A: 5–10 min.	C, H, L	Language Arts Health Technology	Rhyming; vocabulary Basic functions of eyes; health resources Collect information	NCTE 3, 4 AAHE 1, 2 ISTE 5
Clear Sailing	P: 15 min. A: 15 min.	C, H, L	Health Language Arts Art	Basic functions of eyes Read to develop empathy; use print to communicate Use art materials to retell story; fine motor	AAHE 1 NCTE 1, 5 MENC 1

P: Approximate Preparation Time   **A:** Approximate Activity Time   **C:** Classroom Activity

H: Home Activity   **L:** Library Activity

Baby Duck and the Bad Eyeglasses by Amy Hest

Glasses for Fun

Use this fingerplay to introduce some of the reasons why people wear glasses. It's a perfect introduction to the story of *Baby Duck and the Bad Eyeglasses.*

Supplies:

◆ None

Preparation:

◆ None

Activity:

Make two circles with the thumb and forefinger of each hand. Hold these circles in front of your eyes like glasses. Do this for each character as you recite the fingerplay. Add gestures as indicated.

Grandma wears glasses so she can see.   *(Turn head from side to side.)*

Daddy wears glasses to read.   *(Put hands palm up as if reading a book. Flip right hand as if turning pages.)*

Brother wears glasses to keep out the sun.   *(Pretend to shield eyes from the sun.)*

I wear glasses just for fun!   *(Great big smile!)*

Discussion:

What are some reasons people wear glasses?

How do sunglasses help people see better?

How do reading glasses help people?

Do you ever wear pretend glasses just for fun?

Read *Baby Duck and the Bad Eyeglasses* to the children.

Tech Tie-In:

◆ www.dada.it/eyeweb/ealbin.htm

Log onto this Web site to let children practice an eye test designed just for them. The Random E test prepares children for the procedure. Preview the site before conducting the tests.

54

Baby Duck and the Bad Eyeglasses by Amy Hest

Clear Sailing

Children can make a pair of red glasses just like Baby Duck's. After they try them on, they can compare what Baby Duck saw before and after she got her new glasses.

Supplies:

- One copy of Make "Pretend" Glasses reproducible
- One red chenille stem for each child plus two extra
- One boat reproducible for each child plus one extra
- One 8" piece of wax paper for each child plus one extra
- Crayons
- Mirror
- Optional: one skein of yarn

Preparation:

- Make a sample pair of glasses by following the illustrated instructions on the reproducible.
- Print your name on the larger boat in the reproducible. Color the picture, but do not color over the area where your name is printed on the boat.
- Put the wax paper aside to hand out when the children have finished making their glasses and coloring their handout.

Discussion:

(Ask after completing the activity.)

What did Baby Duck think about her glasses when she looked in the mirror?

What was Baby Duck's biggest worry? *(Her glasses would fall off.)*

What could Baby Duck do after she got her glasses that she couldn't do before? *(see clearly)*

Was it easier to read your name when the wax paper was held above the boat or when the wax paper was laid on top of the boat?

Which way was most like what Baby Duck saw before she got her new glasses?

Do you know anyone who wears glasses?

How would you feel if you needed to wear glasses to see?

Activity:

1. Read *Baby Duck and the Bad Eyeglasses* while wearing the sample pair of glasses.

2. Tell the children they will make a pretend pair of glasses just like the ones Baby Duck wore in the story. Then they will compare how things looked to Baby Duck before she got her glasses and after she got her glasses.

3. Using a chenille stem, show the children each step in making their pretend glasses. Help them complete their glasses. (As an alternative, have the glasses prepared in advance.)

4. Give each child a turn looking in the mirror to size up their glasses just as Baby Duck did.

5. Ask children to print their names with a black or dark crayon on the top of the larger boat in the reproducible.

6. Have them color the rest of the picture except the part of the boat with their name.

7. Give each child a piece of wax paper. Have the children hold the wax paper three or four inches above their drawing. Ask them to read their name.

8. Now have them lay the wax paper on top of their handout and put on their glasses. (They may have to hold their glasses to their face if they are unable to get them to stay on.)

9. Have them try to read their name again.

10. Optional: Tie a long piece of yarn to the top of each lens so the glasses can hang around the child's neck when not being worn. This is how Grampa Duck wore his glasses.

11. Have the children take their glasses home to share the story of Baby Duck with their families.

Tech Tie-In:

Take a digital photograph of the children wearing their eyeglasses. Publish it on the school Web site with the caption, "Visionary Class Read's *Baby Duck and the Bad Eyeglasses.*"

Make "Pretend" Glasses

Show the children how to bend the chenille stem following the instructions below.

1. Hold the stem vertically. Make the top part of the capital "B." Leave some extra to wrap around the straight part of the stem below the top of the "B."

2. Wrap the extra around the straight part of the stem.

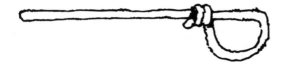

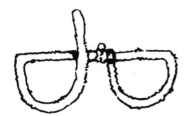

3. Make the bottom part of the capital "B." Leave some extra to wrap around the stem. If the bottom of the "B" is a lot bigger or smaller than the top part of the "B," slide the top part of the "B" up or down to make them about the same size.

4. Wrap the extra around the straight part of the chenille stem.

5. Wear the glasses.

Boat Reproducible

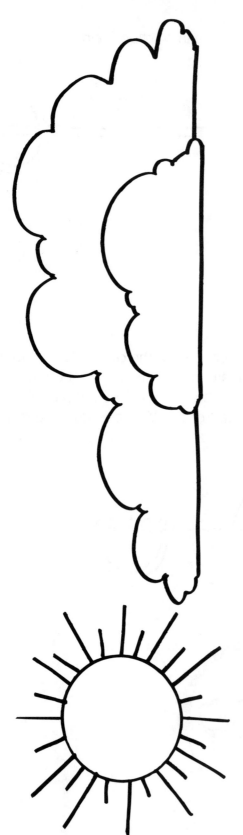

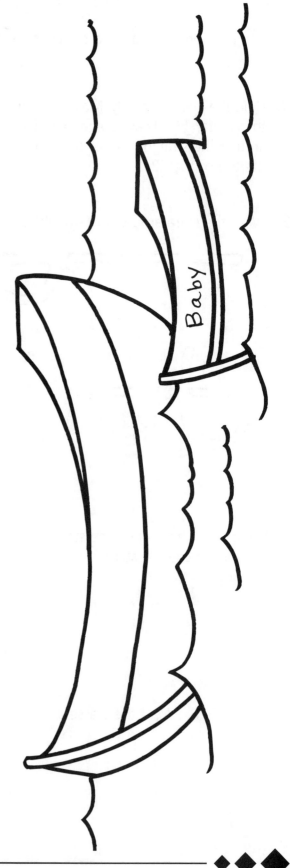

Baby

Bark, George
by Jules Feiffer

Feiffer, Jules, *Bark, George*. HarperCollins, 1999, 32 pp., 0-06-205185-7

George's mother is so frustrated. Every time she tries to get George to bark, he makes the sound of another animal instead. She takes him to the vet. The vet reaches deep inside George and pulls out one animal after another, until at last he puts on his longest latex glove and pulls out a cow. Now when the vet tells George to bark he says, "Arf!"

George's mother is thrilled. On the way home she wants to show George off, but when she tells him to bark he says, "Hello!"

◆ Skills Table ◆

Activity	Time	Location	Subjects	Skills	Standards
Out With It	P: 15 min. A: 15 min.	C, H, L	Language Arts Math Art Health	Story recall Sequencing Fine motor; art processes Listening skills	NCTE 3 NCTM 2 MENC-A1 AAHE 5
Is There a Doctor in the House?	P: 40 min. A: 10–15 min.	C, H, L	Language Arts Science Math Health Technology	Story recall Use senses to compare objects Sequencing Listening skills Communication	NCTE 3 NAS- B NCTM 2 AAHE 5 ISTE 4

P: Approximate Preparation Time **A:** Approximate Activity Time **C:** Classroom Activity
H: Home Activity **L:** Library Activity

Out With It

Retell the story of George by pulling the animals from his mouth in the correct order. Children can make their own George to take home and share with their families.

Supplies:

◆ One double-sided copy of dog reproducibles for each child plus one extra

◆ One copy of story strip reproducible for each child plus one extra

◆ One 3½" x 7" construction paper strip for each child plus one extra

◆ Glue sticks

◆ Children's scissors

◆ Crayons

◆ Clear adhesive tape

◆ Ruler

◆ Scissors

Preparation:

◆ Color and cut out the dog.

◆ Cut slits on the back of the dog where indicated.

◆ Tape the strip of construction paper on the back of the dog where marked. Tape the long edges only.

◆ Color and cut out the animals and sound squares. Cut out the strip along the dotted lines.

◆ Glue the animals on the strip from left to right in the same order the vet pulled them from George.

◆ Flip over the strip and glue the sounds in the same order.

◆ Slide the story strip into the dog's construction paper sleeve so that when the dog is turned over the strip can be pulled from its mouth to retell the story. Start with the animal side.

Discussion:

(Ask after reading the book to the children.)

How do you think George's mother felt when George couldn't bark?

Do the pictures give you clues about how she felt?

Is this story real or pretend?

How do you know?

Show the children the sample dog.

In what order did the vet pull the animals from George?

Pull the strip as the children recall the order. Tell the children that the story starts on the left.

Turn the strip over and reinsert it in the sleeve so the animal sounds are visible.

What is this sound?

What animal makes this sound?

Continue asking the children to match the sound with the animal as you pull through each frame of the strip.

Tell the children they will be making their own dog like George.

Will you glue the first picture on the left or right side of the strip of paper? (Point to the left and right sides.)

Why?

Activity:

1. Have children make their own dogs by explaining each of the steps noted in the preparation section.

2. Assist in cutting the slits and taping the strips to the back of the dog.

3. Help children glue the pictures and words onto the strip from the left side to the right side.

4. Encourage children to take their dogs home and use both the pictures and words to retell the story to their families.

Tech Tie-In:

Encourage children to visit their local public library to find a copy of *Bark, George*. The information, of course, is on the back of their dog.

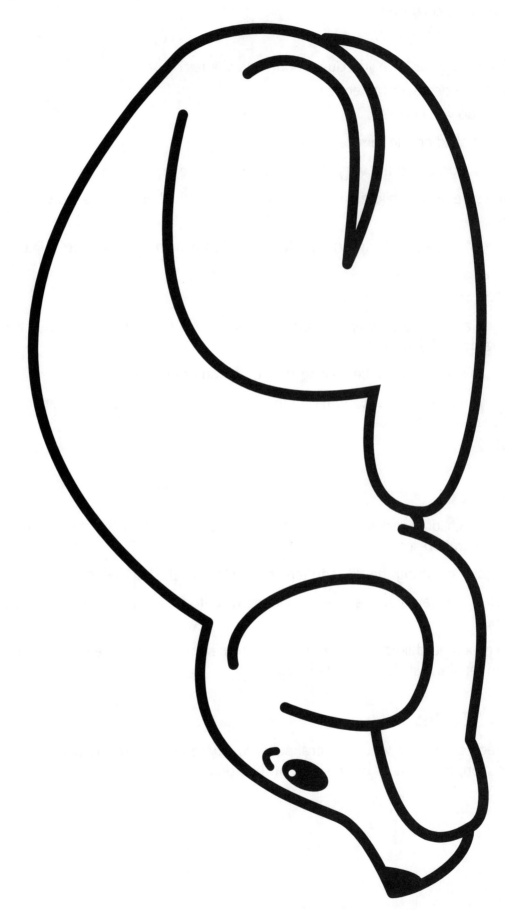

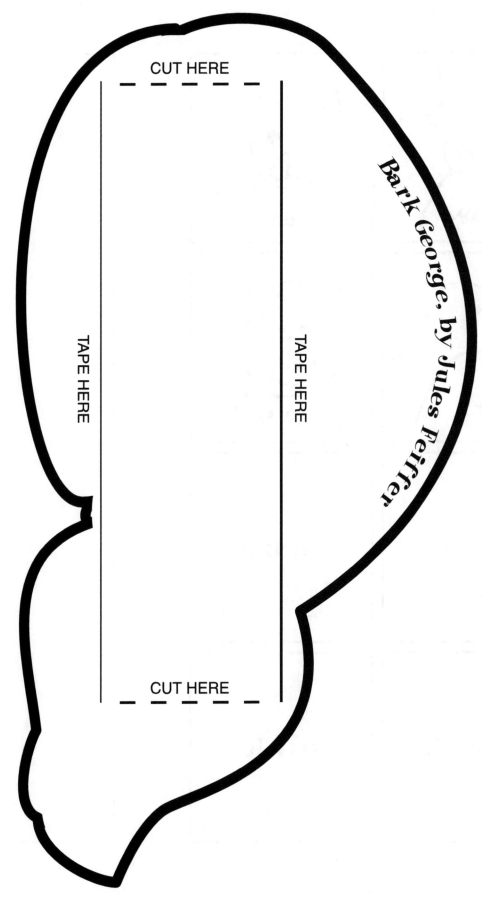

CUT HERE

TAPE HERE

TAPE HERE

Bark George, by Jules Feiffer

CUT HERE

64

Is There a Doctor in the House?

Retell the story by letting children take turns as the vet. Using their sense of touch, they can pull out the animal making each sound.

Supplies:

- Empty oatmeal container (18 oz.) or other similar sized container

- Adult tube sock: brown, black or white

- Black 1" pompom

- Two 14 mm wiggle eyes

- Square of black felt

- Construction paper

- Optional: Other small plastic animals or items that make sounds (bell, phone, or alarm clock)

- One copy of the cow, pig, duck and cat reproducible from the "Out With It" activity

- One each: small plastic cat, duck, pig, cow

- Crayons

- Scissors

- Glue stick

- Glue gun and hot glue

Preparation:

- Pull the sock over the empty container so that the opening of the sock droops over the opening of the container. This is the dog's face.

- With a hot glue gun, attach the pompom nose to the top of the sock, near the edge. Glue the wiggle eyes above the nose.

- Cut two felt ears about 3" long and glue on either side of the "face."

- Enlarge the animal reproducible. Cut apart and color the animals. Mount each one on a piece of construction paper.

Discussion:

(Ask after reading the story to the children.)

Can you name the animals in the same order the vet pulled them out of George?

If you couldn't see the animals, could you still guess what they were by hearing the sounds they made?

How are the animals the vet pulled from George alike?

How are they different?

Activity:

1. Have the children hold and look at each animal carefully. Then ask them to do the same with their eyes closed and guess which animal they are holding.

2. Review the order of the animals as they were pulled from George by showing these pages from the book.

3. Have children take turns being the vet and vet's assistant.

4. When the vet asks George to bark, the assistant will hold up the picture of the first animal pulled from George. As each animal is held up, all of the group except the vet will make the sound of that animal.

5. The vet must use his/her sense of touch to reach inside George and pull out the correct animal.

6. Choose different children to play the part of the vet and the vet's assistant each time an animal is pulled from George.

Variations:

◆ Easy: Complete the activity using only one plastic animal at a time inside George.

◆ Hard: Eliminate the first activity step and picture clues and include animals or objects not in the story. After you make a sound, the class can guess the animal or object before the vet pulls that animal or object out of the dog.

Tech Tie-In:

◆ www.ci.shrewsbury.ma.us/Sps/Schools/Beal/Curriculum/critterclinic/critterclinic.html

Visit this Web site, part of the Beal Early Childhood Center in Shrewsbury, Massachusetts. Link to the wonderful animal-related activities and take a virtual field trip of a local veterinary clinic, vet tools, vet jobs, and pet care. Be sure to click on Critter Clinic to see the actual clinic that is set up permanently at the school for teachers and students to use throughout the day. There are great ideas here for a teacher or librarian's own Web page.

◆ www.uga.edu/~lam/kids/

Follow cats and a dog through a typical vet checkup on this Web site run by the College of Veterinary Medicine at the University of Georgia. Text is age appropriate. *(College students maintain this site, though, so the online vet portion of the site is not always available.)*

Gregory the Terrible Eater
by Mitchell Sharmat

Sharmat, Mitchell, *Gregory the Terrible Eater*.
Scholastic, 1980, 32 pp., 0-590-07586-1

Gregory is such a terrible eater. He wants only fruit, vegetables, eggs, fish, and other disgusting things. He refuses to eat all the good things his parents offer him, like bottle caps and tin cans.

His parents take him to Dr. Ram, who recommends introducing new foods to Gregory slowly. It works and soon Gregory is eating everything, including his father's necktie and his mother's sewing basket. Luckily, Gregory's parents find a way to cure Gregory's eating problem and he learns to eat just the right combination of things.

◆ Skills Table ◆

Activity	Time	Location	Subjects	Skills	Standards
Check It Out	P: 45 min. A: 15–20 min.	C, H, L	Math Economics Language Arts Health Technology	Observe details; classify Identify jobs Use spoken language to communicate clearly Identify food groups Collect information	NCTM 2,5 NCEE 6 NCTE 4 AAHE 3 ISTE 5
We're Going to the Grocery Store	P: 20 min. A: 10–15 min.	C, L	Language Arts Music Technology	Vocabulary; use spoken language to communicate clearly Sing in groups Collect & evaluate information	NCTE 4 MENC-M1 ISTE 5

P: Approximate Preparation Time   **A:** Approximate Activity Time   **C:** Classroom Activity
H: Home Activity   **L:** Library Activity

Gregory the Terrible Eater by Mitchell Sharmat

Check It Out

When a goat is a grocery store sacker, he needs all the help he can get, especially when his customers want their purchases sorted by food group. Luckily those customers will be able to help since they will be learning about the food pyramid with this activity.

Supplies:

- One adult knit sock, tan or gray
- Two 1.5 cm wiggle eyes
- Small piece of polyester fiberfill for the goat's beard
- Paper plate
- Two pieces of felt: black and red
- Food Groups reproducible
- Food Guide Pyramid reproducible
- Goat horn, ear and mouth pattern
- Glue gun and hot glue
- Glue stick

- Construction paper
- Six lunch bags
- Grocery story newspaper ads with items from each food group
- Scissors
- Crayons
- White chalk
- Scrap paper

Preparation:

- Color and cut out the food groups reproducible. Glue each picture to a brown paper lunch bag.
- Cut out grocery ad pictures of foods from all five food groups. Each child should have at least one. Glue to construction paper squares cut slightly larger than the pictures. Laminate.

To Make the Puppet:

- Using the goat puppet patterns, cut two ears from black felt and the mouth from red felt.
- Cut one horn from the grooved edge of the paper plate. Flip the pattern over before cutting the second horn. Turn the horns over so the back side of the plate is facing up. Fold up 1" of the base of the horns.

◆ Stuff the foot of the sock loosely with newspaper.

Important: The bottom of the sock will become the top of the puppet with the heel on the back of the puppeteer's hand, not the palm of the hand.

◆ Glue the mouth to the top of the sock. Center it where the largest end of the oval is touching the stitching across the toe of the sock.

◆ Remove the newspaper and place the puppet on your hand. Bending your fingers down, mark the eye locations by centering two chalk marks at the base of your fingers, just above the knuckles. The eyes will be glued here later.

◆ Remove the puppet from your hand. Make two chalk marks ¾" above the eye marks. This is where the horns should be attached. Make one chalk mark 1¼" below the bottom of the mouth to indicate beard placement.

◆ Stuff the foot of the sock loosely with newspaper. Hot glue eyes and horns. The fold of the horn should be lined up with the mark so that it touches the sides of the sock.

◆ Glue the ears over the bent part of the horns.

◆ Glue a small piece of fiberfill on the chalk mark indicating placement of the beard. Trim the beard with scissors to make it slightly pointed at the bottom.

Discussion:

(Ask after introducing Greg the Grocery Store Goat)

What are the five food groups?

How is the Fats & Sweets group different from the other groups of foods in the Food Pyramid?

Can you think of some foods that could belong in more than one food group? (pizza, hamburger)

What jobs do the cashier and the sacker at the grocery store do?

Does a real grocery store sacker sort the food into the bags by food group?

How does the sacker decide what to put in each bag?

Activity:

(Complete after reading the book to the children.)

1. Show the children the food group pictures. Ask them to name some of the foods in each group.

2. Show the children the Food Guide Pyramid. Discuss the kinds of food that belong in each food group.

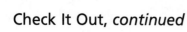

3. Introduce Greg the Grocery Store Goat and explain that his job is to bag items by food group.

4. Give each child a food item from the grocery store ads. Explain that Greg will need their help when he bags their groceries. They must tell him the kind of food they purchased and its food group so he can put the item in the correct sack.

5. Choose one child at a time to give his/her food item to Greg. If a child is having difficulty with the task, let Greg help give the answers. If a food fits in more than one group, let the children decide what group they would put it in.

6. After all the food items are in the bags, empty one bag at a time and have the children repeat each food name, and finally the food group.

7. Complete the discussion section.

8. Save the grocery store ads for the We're Going to the Grocery Store activity.

Tech Tie-In:

◆ http://www.usda.gov/cnpp/KidsPyra/

Visit the USDA Web site to download the handout, posters, or a booklet with tips for using the Food Guide Pyramid for Young Children. The food guide pyramid in this activity is used with permission from the United States Department of Agriculture.

◆ Give children copies of the food guide pyramid to share with their families. Have them keep a daily record of the food groups included in their meals at home. They can bring the records to the library to maintain a digital diary. After one week, have the children review their digital diary entries and compare with the food guide pyramid.

Gregory the Terrible Eater by Mitchell Sharmat

FOOD Guide PYRAMID

for Young Children

A Daily Guide for 2- to 6-Year-Olds

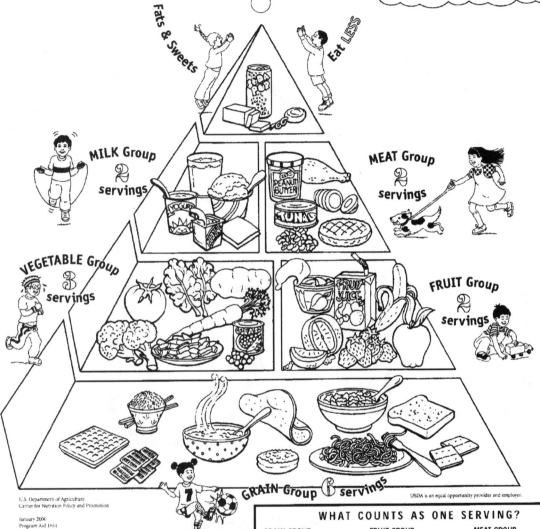

Fats & Sweets — Eat LESS

MILK Group 2 servings

MEAT Group 2 servings

VEGETABLE Group 3 servings

FRUIT Group 2 servings

GRAIN Group 6 servings

U.S. Department of Agriculture
Center for Nutrition Policy and Promotion

January 2000
Program Aid 1651

USDA is an equal opportunity provider and employer.

FOOD IS FUN and learning about food is fun, too. Eating foods from the Food Guide Pyramid and being physically active will help you grow healthy and strong.

WHAT COUNTS AS ONE SERVING?

GRAIN GROUP
1 slice of bread
1/2 cup of cooked rice or pasta
1/2 cup of cooked cereal
1 ounce of ready-to-eat cereal

VEGETABLE GROUP
1/2 cup of chopped raw or cooked vegetables
1 cup of raw leafy vegetables

FRUIT GROUP
1 piece of fruit or melon wedge
3/4 cup of juice
1/2 cup of canned fruit
1/4 cup of dried fruit

MILK GROUP
1 cup of milk or yogurt
2 ounces of cheese

MEAT GROUP
2 to 3 ounces of cooked lean meat, poultry, or fish.

1/2 cup of cooked dry beans, or 1 egg counts as 1 ounce of lean meat. 2 tablespoons of peanut butter count as 1 ounce of meat.

FATS AND SWEETS
Limit calories from these.

Four- to 6-year-olds can eat these serving sizes. Offer 2- to 3-year-olds less, except for milk.
Two- to 6-year-old children need a total of 2 servings from the milk group each day.

EAT a variety of FOODS AND ENJOY!

71

Goat Puppet Patterns

A Food Group Reproducible

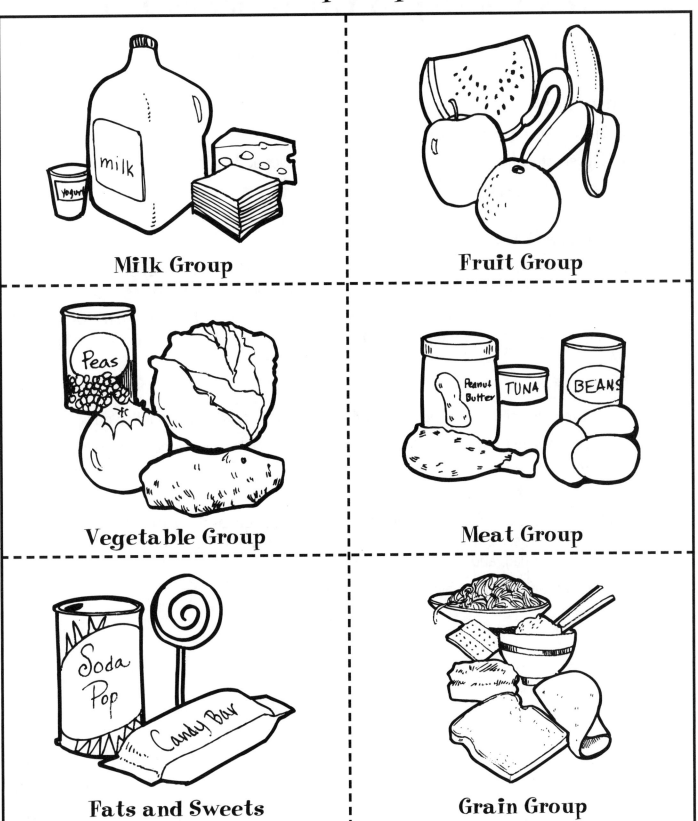

Milk Group

Fruit Group

Vegetable Group

Meat Group

Fats and Sweets

Grain Group

Gregory the Terrible Eater by Mitchell Sharmat

We're Going to the Grocery Store

Let children sing about their purchases as they shop for groceries.

Supplies:

◆ Brown paper grocery bag

◆ Grocery store newspaper ads from the Check It Out activity

◆ Construction paper

Preparation:

◆ Collect the grocery store newspaper ads from the Check It Out activity or cut out pictures from the newspaper grocery store ads to represent all the food groups.

◆ Glue on small pieces of construction paper cut slightly larger than each ad (if not already prepared from the Check It Out activity).

Activity:

1. Give each child a food picture. Say the name of the food as it is handed out.

2. Sing "We're Going to the Grocery Store" as each child says the name of his/her food item and drops it in your shopping bag.

3. Have children stand to sing the first verse.

4. Choose the children by touching them on the shoulder as the verse is sung. During the second verse, have children sing the name of their food, place it in the shopping bag, and return to their seats.

5. Sing the final verse while everyone is seated. Repeat.

We're Going to the Grocery Store
(Sing to the tune of "She'll Be Coming Round the Mountain")

1. Oh, we're going to the grocery store today,
   We're going to the grocery store today.
   Oh, we're going to the grocery store,
   We're going to the grocery store,
   We're going to the grocery store today.

2. We'll buy _____ and _____ today,
   We'll buy _____ and _____ today,
   We'll buy _____ and _____, _____, and _____,
   We'll buy _____ and _____ today.

3. Oh, we'll take all our good food home to eat, Yum, Yum!
   We'll take all our good food home to eat, Yum, Yum!
   Oh, we'll cook it up and have a feast,
   We'll be sure to save YOU a piece,
   We'll take all our good food home to eat, Yum, Yum!

Variation:

Sing the song without using the pictures or the grocery bag. As you point to children throughout the song they will name a food.

Tech Tie-In:

◆ http://www.childrenssoftware.com/lc/funfood

   Check out these fun food recipes on the Internet. This Web page is a link on the Little Clickers Web page. Little Clickers sites are recommended by the Children's Software & New Media Revue as safe, developmentally appropriate sites for kids.

◆ As a group, select items from the grocery store ads to create a meal. Develop a computerized menu using the selections. Let each child select or design his/her own images to include on the menu. Print out menus for the children to take home for a family meal treat.

   Add recipes from the Little Clickers Web page to accompany the menu.

Make Way for Ducklings

JUV
398.8
M 12m

By Robert McCloskey

McCloskey, Robert, *Make Way for Ducklings*. Viking, 1941, 65 pp., 0-670-45149-5

Mr. and Mrs. Mallard want to find just the right place to raise their babies. They finally choose a little island in the Charles River, not too far from the Public Garden where they can follow the swan boats and eat peanuts.

The large, pencil drawings of the ducks and the timeless story continue to please children, just as they did in 1942 when this book won the Caldecott Medal.

◆ Skills Table ◆

Activity	Time	Location	Subjects	Skills	Standards
Home Sweet Home	P: 20 min. A: 10–15 min.	C, H, L	Science Language Arts Technology	Animal habitats Story recall; interpret text Use technology to create product	NAS-C NCTE 3 ISTE 3
Watch Your Step	P: 20 min. A: 15 min.	C, L	Health Art	Identify responsible health behaviors; compare safe and risky behaviors Select and evaluate subject matter and symbols	AAHE 3 MENC-A3

P: Approximate Preparation Time   **A:** Approximate Activity Time   **C:** Classroom Activity
H: Home Activity   **L:** Library Activity

Make Way for Ducklings by Robert McCloskey

Home Sweet Home

Children can review what they learned about Mr. and Mrs. Mallard's choice of homes and apply their knowledge in a computer activity.

Supplies:

◆ Flannel Board

◆ Yarn in color that contrasts with flannel board

◆ Copy of flannel board reproducible

◆ Felt square

◆ Crayons

◆ Scissors

◆ Glue stick

◆ Optional: Computer with Kidspiration® software for Tech Tie-In activity

Preparation:

◆ Color, cut, and laminate each picture on the reproducible.

◆ Glue a small piece of felt to the back of each picture.

◆ Cut a piece of yarn equal to ⅔ the height of the flannel board. Place it on the flannel board to divide it in half vertically, forming two columns.

Discussion:

(Ask after reading the book to the children.)

What were the things Mr. and Mrs. Mallard wanted their home to have?
Why?
What were the things Mr. and Mrs. Mallard did not want their home to have?
Why not?
Did the Mallard family's first home on the island in the Charles River have everything that they liked?
Was there anything they didn't like?
Why did they decide to live in the Public Garden even though there were bicycles?

Would it be more difficult to be a duck living in the city or one living in the country? Why?

What other books does this story remind you of?

Activity:

1. Place the happy face above one column of the flannel board. Place the sad face above the other column.

2. Hold up one picture at a time. Ask children to decide in which column Mr. and Mrs. Mallard would have placed the picture.

3. They should put the picture of the fish, peanut, water and island on the Happy Face side of the flannel board. The fox, turtle and bicycle should be on the Sad Face side of the flannel board.

4. Ask the children to list other things that could be added to either column.

Variation:

In place of the flannel board, set up the software as noted in the Tech Tie-In on a video projector to create the above activity.

Tech Tie-In:

◆ www.inspiration.com.

Download a 30-day trial program of Kidspiration® from this site and set up the activity:

Use the SuperGrouper tool to make two "backyard" bins. Title one Happy Duck and one Sad Duck.

Use the happy face and picture of the duckling to illustrate the Happy Duck bin. Use the sad face and picture of the duckling to illustrate the Sad Duck bin.

Use the teacher menu and save this as an activity in the science category. Type these directions over the appropriate bin:

Click and drag pictures of things Mr. and Mrs. Mallard wanted into the Happy Duck bin.

Click and drag pictures of things Mr. and Mrs. Mallard did not want into the Sad Duck bin.

Note: There is no picture of a peanut, so let children choose another picture that tells the same story.

Happy Face, Sad Face
Flannel Board Reproducibles

sad

happy

bicycle

fish

turtle

island

fox

peanuts

water

Make Way for Ducklings by Robert McCloskey

Watch Your Step

Reinforce pedestrian safety tips by reviewing the lessons taught by Mrs. Mallard.

Supplies:

- Duck reproducible
- Bulletin board paper
- Drawing paper
- Crayons

Preparation:

- Enlarge one copy of the duck to make the mother duck. Make eight copies the size of the original reproducible to represent the ducklings. Color.
- Print the book title and author on the mother duck.
- Print "Watch out for cars and things with wheels!" on the ducklings, one word per duckling.
- Mount ducks on bulletin board paper in a line behind the mother duck to display the slogan.
- Copy the Pedestrian Safety Rules onto the board.

Pedestrian Safety Rules

1. Walk on the sidewalk if you can.
2. If there is no sidewalk, walk facing traffic.
3. Wear light colored clothing or reflective material at night.
4. Look both ways before crossing streets.
5. Walk when you cross a street. Do not run.
6. Cross the street at a corner or crosswalk.

Note: Before reading the story, ask the children to pay special attention to all the things the ducklings learned from their mother.

Discussion:

(Ask after reading the story to the children.)

What are the things Mrs. Mallard taught the ducklings?

Which of those things have you learned at home or at school?

Why are safety rules important?

Name some safety rules at school.

Name some safety rules at home.

Introduce the meaning of pedestrian, a person who is walking. Mrs. Mallard and her ducklings were like pedestrians.

Activity:

1. Introduce the Pedestrian Safety Rules.

2. Have children give examples for each rule.

3. After all the rules are discussed, have children draw a picture of one of the rules they follow when they are walking. Make sure all of the rules are represented by at least one child.

4. Ask the children to present their pictures and tell the group what rule it represents.

5. Print the rule below each picture.

6. Hang the pictures under the duck banner.

Tech Tie-In:

◆ Arrange for a telephone conference call with a law enforcement officer on the importance of following the pedestrian safety rules.

Have each child tell about the safety rule he/she illustrated. Remind the children that the officer cannot see their pictures, so they will have to describe them.

The officer can ask follow-up questions to reinforce the rules.

A Duck Pattern

Max Cleans Up
by Rosemary Wells

Wells, Rosemary, *Max Cleans Up*. Viking, 2000, 24 pp., 0-0670-89218-1

Ruby has decided it's time for Max to clean up his room. While Ruby cleans and organizes, Max retrieves his treasures from the trash and puts them in his pocket. Anything else he thinks she might throw away goes in his pocket as well. When Ruby has his room completely organized she makes the mistake of asking Max what is in his pocket, and with a mischievous grin he shows her.

◆ Skills Table ◆

Activity	Time	Location	Subjects	Skills	Standards
Shape Up	P: 30 min. A: 10–15 min.	C, H, L	Math Science Technology	Sort by color, shape and size; problem solving Scientific inquiry skills; describe properties of objects Develop positive attitudes toward technology	NCTM 3, 6 NAS- A,B ISTE 2

P: Approximate Preparation Time **A:** Approximate Activity Time **C:** Classroom Activity
H: Home Activity **L:** Library Activity

Shape Up

What kinds of things are hidden in the pocket of these colorful overalls? Children can find many ways to organize the red, yellow, and blue shapes as they classify by color, shape, and size.

Supplies:

◆ One expanding file pocket

◆ Red plaid fabric

◆ One sheet of white poster board

◆ Three snack-size plastic bags

◆ Construction paper: red, yellow and blue

◆ Stapler

◆ Scissors

◆ Glue stick

◆ Clear adhesive tape

◆ Markers

Preparation:

◆ Print "Shape Up" at the top of the long edge of the poster board.

◆ Cut and glue a piece of red plaid fabric on the front of the file pocket.

◆ Staple the file pocket on the right hand side of the poster board to create Max's pocket. This should be child height and secure so that children can reach inside.

◆ Tape three plastic snack bags on the left side of the poster board, one above the other. Tape so that the bags can be opened and closed.

◆ Use the patterns and construction paper to cut one each of the following:

    Red: large square, medium triangle, small circle

    Blue: large circle, medium square, small triangle

    Yellow: large triangle, medium circle, small square

◆ Laminate and place in the file pocket.

Discussion:

(Ask after reading the book to the children.)

What are some of the ways Ruby sorted Max's things when she helped him clean up his room?

Are there any other ways she could have sorted them?

How do you organize things in your room?

Can things be sorted by color, shape and size?

Activity:

1. Show the children the shapes, in the mystery pocket one at a time.

2. As the children name the color, shape, and size of each one, place the shape in the pocket.

3. Give each child a turn at drawing a shape from the mystery pocket.

4. Have them sort the shapes by size: large shapes in the top snack bag, medium shapes in the middle bag and small shapes in the bottom bag.

5. Repeat the activity, sorting by color and shape.

Tech Tie-In:

◆ www.rosemarywells.com

Visit Rosemary Wells' Web page to print out coloring pages of Max and Ruby. Children can also take turns playing a memory game.

Shape Up Patterns

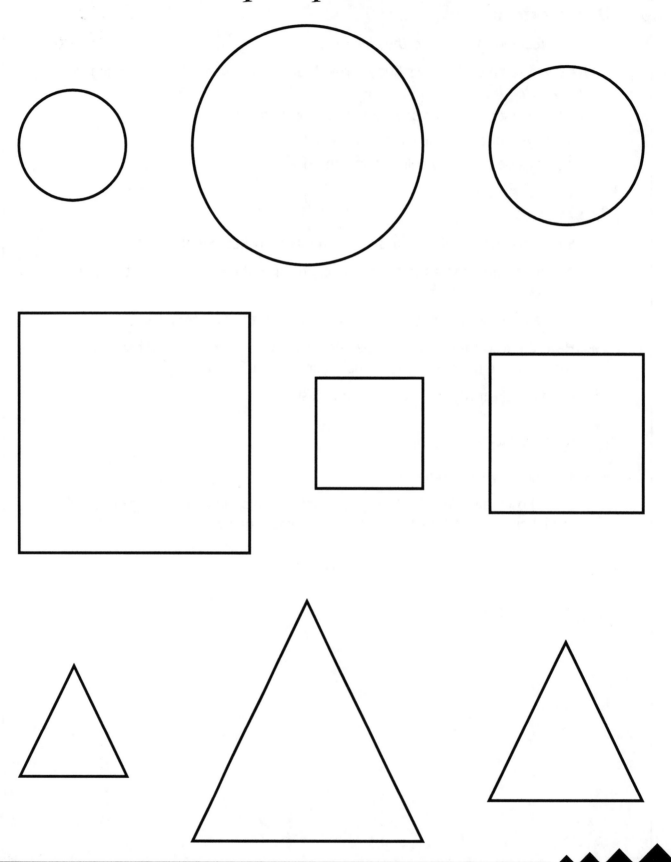

A Pocket for Corduroy

JUV
F855p

by Don Freeman

Freeman, Don, *A Pocket for Corduroy*. Viking, 1978, 32 pp., 0-670-56172-X

In this second book about Corduroy, the little bear discovers that there are some things a bear needs for his overalls besides a button. While he is at the laundromat with Lisa and her mother, he notices Lisa taking everything out of her pockets before her clothes are washed. Corduroy goes in search of a pocket and ends up spending the night at the laundromat. When Lisa returns for him the next day, he tells her he was searching for a pocket, so she makes him one and includes a card with his name tucked inside.

◆ Skills Table ◆

Activity	Time	Location	Subjects	Skills	Standards
Pocket Power	P: 40 min. A: 10–15 min.	C, L	Math	Understand numbers	NCTM 1
			Geography	Matching addresses	NGS 4
			Health	Understanding feelings, facial expressions	AAHE 5
			Info. Literacy	Appreciate literature and other creative forms of information	ALA 5
			Technology	Compare and evaluate print and electronic media	ISTE 5

P: Approximate Preparation Time **A:** Approximate Activity Time **C:** Classroom Activity
H: Home Activity **L:** Library Activity

Pocket Power

The four bears in this game need help finding their way home. Luckily they have address cards tucked inside their pockets.

Supplies:

◆ Four copies of bear reproducible

◆ Four copies of overalls reproducible

◆ Four copies of house reproducible

◆ Construction paper: four brown; one red, blue, green and orange

◆ Scissors

◆ White school glue

◆ Permanent black marker

◆ Four ¾" brass paper fasteners

◆ Crayons

◆ Four 10" x 13" manila envelopes

◆ Four bookends

◆ Two unlined 3" x 5" index cards

Preparation:

Making the Bears:

◆ Trace and cut four sets of bear body parts from brown construction paper.

◆ Trace and cut one pair of overalls and one rectangle from each color of construction paper: red, blue, green, and orange.

◆ Trace and cut four circles from one manila folder. Label with the facial expressions as shown on the pattern.

◆ Glue a rectangle pocket in a contrasting color to the front of each pair of overalls by applying glue in a thin line around the bottom and sides of the pocket. Do not glue the top edge or middle of the pocket.

◆ Glue the body parts of the bear to the back of the overalls. Use the longest of the two paw patterns for the legs.

◆ Mark the center of the each circle with a pencil. Insert a paper fastener through the nose of each bear, ¼" above the top of the mouth opening. Put the circle on the back of the bear's head. Push the paper fastener through the center of the circle and bend it back to hold the circle onto the bear.

◆ Color the top of the brad and the bear's nose with the black permanent marker. Turn the wheel so that the surprised/scared face is showing.

◆ Draw the details on the bear's face with the black marker as shown on the pattern.

◆ Cut the index cards in half to make four cards. Print a house number and street address at the top of the longest edge of each card. Each card should have different house numbers, but they should all be on the same street. Put a card in each bear's pocket with the address showing.

Making the Houses:

◆ Color the houses different colors. Do not cut out the houses.

◆ Print a house number that matches each of the bears' addresses on the line at the top of each house. Do not write the street name on the houses.

◆ Turn the manila envelopes so that the opening is facing down. Glue one house to the front of each envelope.

◆ The top of the house should be even with the top edge of the envelope. Cut off any of the envelope showing below the bottom of the house.

◆ Slip each envelope over a bookend.

Discussion:

(Ask after reading the book to the children.)

What did Lisa put in Corduroy's pocket?

How would the information in Corduroy's pocket help him get home?

What part of the address is usually on the front of a house?

What is your house number?

Activity:

1. Show the different facial expressions of one bear. Ask the children to describe each of the expressions.

2. Ask the children to decide what the mouth in a straight line means. Neither happy nor sad?

3. Arrange all four bears with the open mouth expression. Tell the children that the bears have just discovered they are lost. Talk about how surprised and scared they look.

4. Select four children. Give each one a bear. Tell them the bears feel better when the children hold them, but they are still not happy. Let them choose the facial expression that best shows how the bears feel.

5. Have each child look at the address card in the bear's pocket and match the bear with the house where it lives.

6. Have each child find the house number that matches the one in the bear's pocket. When the addresses match, have the child holding the bear change the bear's facial expression to a smile.

7. After all of the bears have found their way home, choose four more children to play the game.

8. To increase the difficulty of the game, switch the cards in the bears' pockets before giving them to the next four players.

Tech Tie-In:

◆ Watch this live action video production of *A Pocket for Corduroy*. Compare it to the book. Is there anything you would change in the video?

A Pocket for Corduroy. 1986. 20 minutes. Phoenix/BFA Films and Video, Inc. (470 Park Ave. South, New York, NY 10016)

◆ Using an Internet street guide, let children type in their addresses to search for a map of the street where they live.

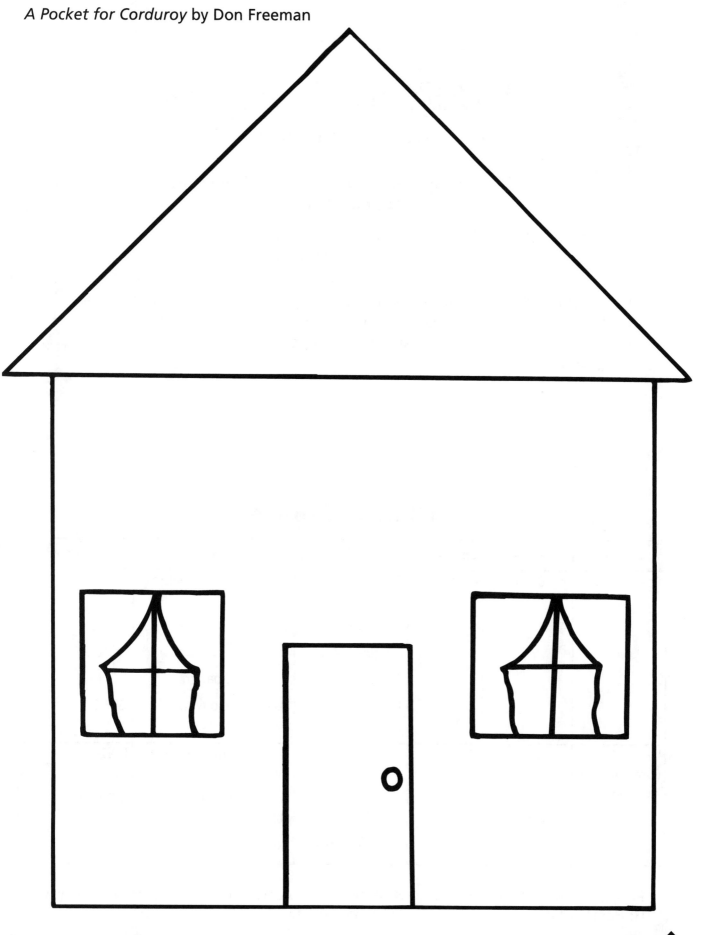

Red-Eyed Tree Frog
by Joy Cowley

Cowley, Joy, *Red-Eyed Tree Frog*. Scholastic, 1999, 32 pp., 0-590-87175-7

Find out what it's like to live in a tropical rainforest, from the perspective of a red-eyed tree frog. This book is informative with incredibly detailed photographs. The close-ups of the tree frog make it seem very large, but the photographs at the end of the book show the actual size of the tree frog. This book succeeds in presenting just the right amount of information for the youngest readers and is a nice nonfiction addition to storytime.

◆ Skills Table ◆

Activity	Time	Location	Subjects	Skills	Standards
Peek-A-Boo	P: 10 min. A: 10 min.	C, H, L	Science Geography Language Arts Math Technology	Camouflage; organisms and their environment Left and right Appreciating rhyme Prediction; patterns Use technology to collect information	NAS-C NGS 2 NCTE 3 NCTM 2 ISTE 5
Watch Out! (Optional Activity)	P: 15 min. A: 10–15 min.	C, H, L	Science Art Language Arts	Environment & animal behavior Use media to retell story; fine motor Read for information	NAS- C MENC-A1 NCTE 1

P: Approximate Preparation Time **A:** Approximate Activity Time **C:** Classroom Activity
H: Home Activity **L:** Library Activity

Peek-A-Boo

Use these simple finger puppets to learn a fun rhyme about the tree frog and reinforce the importance of camouflage in the wild.

Supplies:

◆ Two round green ¾" self-adhesive labels for each child plus two extras

◆ One red paint pen

◆ Optional drawing: Drawing paper
　　　　　　　　　　　Crayons

Preparation:

◆ Use the paint pen to make two red eyes on half of the green sticky dots. Allow time for the paint to dry before the activity.

Discussion:

(Ask after reading the book to the children. Be sure to read the information on the back of the book.)

What does the red-eyed tree frog do that keeps him from being seen?

What shade of green is the red-eyed tree frog when he is afraid?

What color is he when he is not afraid?

What other animals might try to eat the red-eyed tree frog? (boa, bat)

What animals does the red-eyed tree frog eat? (moths, flies, spiders and small grasshoppers)

What time of day does the red-eyed tree frog sleep?

When is he awake?

Activity:

1. Pass out the sticky dots to the children. Have them place the one with the red "eyes" on top of their right thumb and the one without eyes on top of their left thumb.

2. Place your examples on your thumbs in the reverse order, so that when you face the children your frogs match theirs.

3. Show the children how to tuck both thumbs in their fists. Say the rhyme using the indicated gestures. Be prepared to repeat this fun rhyme several times.

Peek·A·Boo

Little tree frog In the tree, With eyes shut tight, He can't be seen.	*Bring left thumb out of fist and fold it over fist so it is visible.* *Put left fist behind back as you shake your head "no."*
Little tree frog With eyes so red, Open them, Jump out of bed!	*Bring right thumb out of fist and fold it over fist so it is visible.* *Pop thumb up in a jumping motion.*

Watch Out! (Optional Activity):

Have children draw a rain forest picture following these steps:

1. Since the red-eyed tree frog wakes up when evening comes to the rain forest, make sure the children color the sky of their picture to look like a sunset.

2. Include at least one predator and one animal that is prey for the red-eyed tree frog.

3. Place finger puppet tree frogs in an appropriate spot on their drawing. Remind them that if their tree frog is not dark green, it is not afraid, so they should be sure to keep it away from any predators in their drawing. They may wish to add legs to their tree frog if its eyes are open since it is just waking up. The tree frog that is asleep should, of course, keep his legs tucked under his body.

4. Display drawings under the heading "Watch Out!"

Tech Tie·In:

◆ http://www.pbs.org/tal/costa_rica/rainwalk.html

Take a self-guided virtual tour of the rainforest. Click on night life to see what other animals besides the red-eyed tree frog are active at night.

Red Leaf, Yellow Leaf JUV E326r
by Lois Ehlert

Ehlert, Lois, *Red Leaf, Yellow Leaf*. Harcourt Brace, 1991, 36 pp., 0-15-266197-2

A little girl tells the story of her tree, from its beginnings as a little maple seed until she and her father finally purchase it at a garden center and plant it in her yard. Children will be attracted to Lois Ehlert's colorful collages, but this is much more than just a pretty book. The story is packed with factual information, and additional notes can be found at the back of the book. There are even directions for making a backyard bird treat.

◆ Skills Table ◆

Activity	Time	Location	Subjects	Skills	Standards
Leaf Dance	P: 30 min.	C, L	Dance	Demonstrate movement skills; communicate meaning	MENC-D1, D3
	A: 5–10 min.		Theatre	Interact in improvisations	MENC- T2
			Language Arts	Interpret texts with a wide range of strategies	NCTE 3
			Science	Describe properties of objects-colors	NAS- B
Tech Tie-In	P: none	C, H, L	Science	Seasons; growth stages of a tree; colors	NAS- C, B, D
	A: 10–15 min.		Theatre	Use props	MENC-T6
			Math	Prediction; patterns	NCTM 2
			Music	Sing in groups	MENC-M1
			Technology	Use technology to promote creativity	ISTE 3

P: Approximate Preparation Time   **A:** Approximate Activity Time   **C:** Classroom Activity
H: Home Activity   **L:** Library Activity

Red Leaf, Yellow Leaf by Lois Ehlert

Leaf Dance

This leaf dance will have children swirling through the room like colorful fall leaves as they act out the poem with hand gestures and body movements. This activity can be done before or after reading the book.

Supplies:

◆ Four pieces each of red, yellow, orange and brown construction paper

◆ Leaf pattern for each child

◆ Clear adhesive tape

Preparation:

◆ Cut and laminate several leaves of each color.

Activity:

1. Ask the children if they have noticed how quietly the leaves fall from the trees in autumn or how the leaves swirl down when the wind blows.

2. Tell the children to follow your gestures as you recite the poem. At the words, "The leaves float softly to the ground," the entire group will float gently and quietly to the floor, just like real leaves.

3. Hold up one paper leaf of each color and have the children say its color name.

4. Tape a leaf to the clothing of each child. Tell them to remember the color of their leaf, because they will have to stop and "freeze" when you name their color.

5. Spread the children evenly across the room.

6. Recite the poem, pausing as you say each color name for each child wearing that color of leaf to freeze. Continue with the last line.

Leaf Dance

The wind blows through the trees so high,   *(Hold arms above head, fingers open. Wave arms and sway body.)*

Dancing leaves across the sky.   *(Lower arms to head level. Wiggle fingers, swirl and sway body.)*

Red, yellow, orange and brown,   *(Children freeze when their color is named.)*

The leaves float softly to the ground.   *(Continue the same motion as hands are lowered to rest in your lap.)*

Tech Tie-In:

Follow these steps to create and sing about the seasons of a tree with this CD. Sesame Street Parent's Magazine voted this one of the six best recordings for the year.

Sing a Song of Seasons. Rachel Buchman, 1997. Rounder Records Corp. (1 Camp Street, Cambridge, MA 02140)

◆ Begin rehearsal by telling the children that you are the tree trunk and they are the branches and leaves.

◆ Create the spring/summer tree by asking all the children with green leaves to gather around the trunk, extending their arms like a tree branch with the leaves at the end.

◆ Repeat for the fall tree with red, yellow, orange and brown leaves.

◆ Have children drop their leaves to create the winter tree.

◆ Have the children repeat the cycles as you sing along with the CD about the seasons.

◆ Encourage them to listen carefully for the cues to their "seasons."

◆ Add a growth cycle by having the tree and branches start with bended knees, straightening them to "grow" with the seasons.

A Leaf Pattern

That's Mine Horace

JUV
K283t

by Holly Keller

Keller, Holly, *That's Mine Horace*. Greenwillow Books, 2000, 24 pp., 0-688-17160-5

When Horace finds a toy truck on the playground that no one claims, he decides to keep it. However, it really belongs to his friend Walter, who tells the teacher that Horace took his truck. Horace denies it, then is unable to face returning to school. After receiving a get well letter from Walter, Horace returns the truck and the two friends find that it is much more fun to share the truck and play together.

◆ Skills Table ◆

Activity	Time	Location	Subjects	Skills	Standards
How Sweet It Is	P: 15 min.	L, C, H	Art	Fine motor coordination; use media to communicate	MENC-A1
	A: 10–15 min.		Health	Sharing-demonstrate ways to show consideration of others; following directions	AAHE 5
			Math	Visualization	NCTM 3

P: Approximate Preparation Time   **A:** Approximate Activity Time   **C:** Classroom Activity
H: Home Activity   **L:** Library Activity

How Sweet It Is

Sharing makes everything sweeter. The two bears in this activity may look like they're fighting over the same cookie, but by unfolding the paper, children can let everyone in on the surprise. The two friends have found that half a cookie is better than a whole cookie if it's shared!

Supplies:

◆ One double-sided bear reproducible for each child plus one extra

◆ Crayons

Preparation:

◆ Print *That's Mine Horace* by Holly Keller on the back on the reproducible. Make the rest of the copies double-sided so the children will be able to let their parents know the title and author of the storytime book.

◆ Fold a sample bear reproducible by following the directions in the activity section.

◆ Do not color the handout, but have a red crayon available to add a smile to the bear's face.

Discussion:

(Ask after reading the book to the children.)

Show the children your sample bear picture. Leave the paper folded so the bears are holding the same cookie.

Do the bears in the picture look happy? (No, they look like they're fighting.)

Unfold the paper. When the paper is opened up, we see the bears are sharing.

How do you think they feel now?

Use the red crayon to change the mouth to a smile. Show the children the words at the bottom of the picture as you read them.

What do you think those words mean?

Activity:

1. Show the children how to fold their paper in half so the bears are facing each other.

2. Then assist them in folding back the picture on the right side of the paper until it looks like the bears are holding onto the same cookie.

3. Have the children use their crayons to draw a smile on the bears, then color the entire picture. Encourage them to take their picture home and show how happy the bears were when they shared. Remind them to show their parents the back of the paper where the title and author of the book is printed.

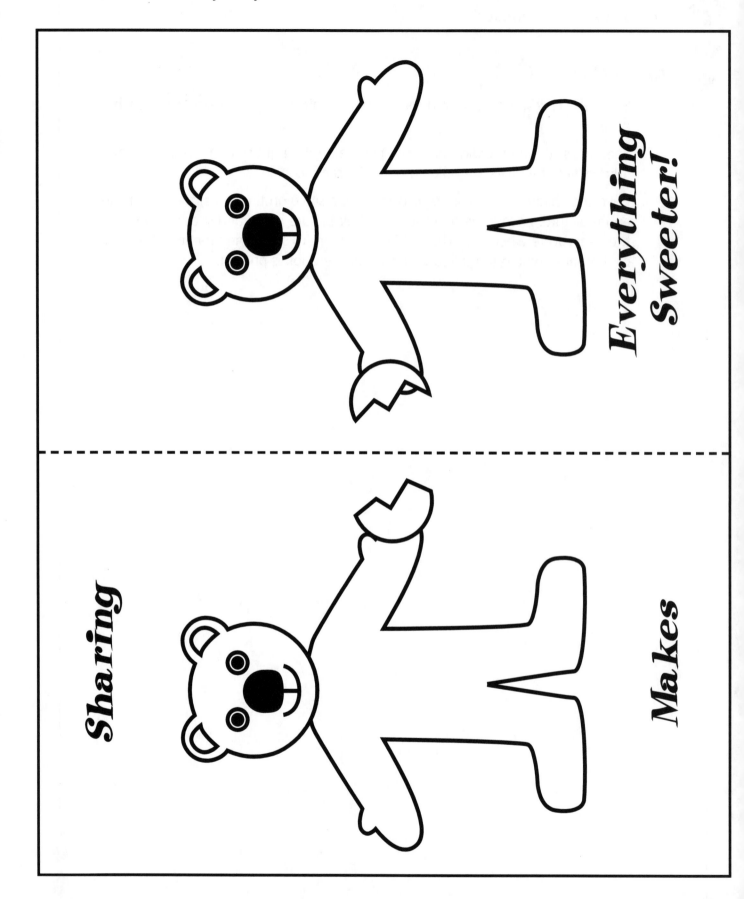

Sharing

Everything
Sweeter!

Makes

The Very Clumsy Click Beetle

JUV
C278vc

by Eric Carle

Carle, Eric, *The Very Clumsy Click Beetle*. Philomel, 1999, 26 pp., 0-399-23201-X

Things aren't always as easy as they look, as the little click beetle in this story finds out. With perseverance, the click beetle finds that he can flip and land on his feet. Like Eric Carle's other books in the "Very" series, this one has lots to attract and hold the attention of young listeners. Bright, colorful paintings and collage make this an excellent storytime choice, but the clicking noise that accompanies the click beetle as he flips through the air will make this book one of the most popular in the library.

◆ Skills Table ◆

Activity	Time	Location	Subjects	Skills	Standards
Practice Makes Perfect	P: 35 min. A: 20–25 min.	C, H, L	Art	Applying media	MENC-A1
			Math	Counting	NCTM 1
			Language Arts	Use strategies to interpret text	NCTE 3
			Science	Characteristics of bugs	NAS-C
			Technology	Use technology tools to enhance learning; interact with experts; collect information	ISTE 3,4,5
It's About Time	P: none A: 15–20 min.	C, H, L	Math	Measuring time	NCTM 4
			Science	Changes in earth and sky	NAS- D
			Art	Communicate meaning; fine motor	MENC-A3
			Technology	Enhance learning; promote creativity	ISTE 3

P: Approximate Preparation Time   **A:** Approximate Activity Time   **C:** Classroom Activity
H: Home Activity   **L:** Library Activity

Practice Makes Perfect

Children will learn the meaning of perseverance as they make their own click beetle and then teach it to flip.

Supplies:

- One plastic spoon for each child plus one extra
- One skein of black yarn
- One package of ¾" assorted color sticky dots
- One package assorted color adhesive paper reinforcements
- Scissors
- One 3" x 5" note card
- Clear adhesive tape
- Black permanent marker
- Optional: Black washable markers

Preparation:

- Precut the yarn for the legs by wrapping black yarn around a 3" x 5" note card. When the note card is full, cut the yarn at both edges of the card so each piece is approximately 3" long. You will need three pieces for each beetle. (If you choose to make the antennae, cut four pieces for each beetle.)
- Stick three pieces of yarn to a short piece of tape, then press it into the spoon bowl to create the legs.
- For antennae, fold a fourth piece of yarn in half and tape it to the underside of the head. If you do not make antennae, be sure to point out this missing feature so the children understand that real beetles have antennae.

Discussion:

Did it take the click beetle more than one try to flip and land right side up? How many tries did it take?

Perseverance means continuing to try to do something even when it is difficult.

Did the click beetle have perseverance?

Do you think the click beetle would have given up?

How many times do you think it will take you to flip the click beetle you make and have it land on its feet?

Name some times when you have persevered. How did you feel when you finally succeeded?

How would you feel if you had given up before you succeeded?

Activity:

Tell the children they are going to make a click beetle they can teach to click and flip. Remind them that it took the click beetle in the book several tries before he managed to flip and land on his feet.

Make the Beetle:

1. Give each child a spoon that has yarn legs attached, approximately nine colored sticky dots and two paper reinforcements.

2. Have each child cover the back of the spoon with his/her own colored sticky dot pattern.

3. Have each child place two paper reinforcements on the back of the beetle.

4. After each child completes his/her beetle, have them bring the beetle to you to add wings and eyes with the permanent black marker. Write the child's initials on the inside of his/her spoon. (As an alternative, provide children with washable markers to let them draw eyes and wings on their own beetles.)

Flip the Beetle:

1. Place the spoon so the back of the beetle rests on the floor or table.

2. Push down on the tip of the spoon bowl and watch the beetle flip. It takes practice to get the beetle to land upright.

Tech Tie-In:

◆ http://bugscope.beckman.uiuc.edu

Schedule an online session to see what real bugs look like from a close-up view through the electron microscope at the University of Illinois at Urbana-Champaign. Bugscope is free for students in grades K–12. A scheduled session allows children to manipulate the electron microscope from an Internet connection in their own school. No registration is required to view other school sessions live, or look at selected electron microscope bug photographs from previous sessions.

It's About Time

Where would you go if you were a click beetle? Let the children use their imaginations while they learn about time in this simple art activity.

Supplies:

◆ One copy of Time-of-Day reproducible for each child

◆ Crayons

◆ Optional: Teaching clock

Preparation:

◆ None

Discussion:

(Ask after reading the book to the children.)

How are the things you do in the morning different from the things you do later in the day?

How did the click beetle's activities change throughout the day?

Do all click beetles do things at the same time of day as the click beetle in the story?

Can you tell if it is morning or afternoon by where the sun is in the sky?

Activity:

1. Give each child a copy of the reproducible. Help children print Morning at the top of the first rectangle, Noon at the top of the second, Evening at the top of the third, and Night at the top of the fourth (or use pictures only).

2. Have children draw pictures in each of the rectangles to show the click beetle as he goes throughout his day.

3. Ask the children if their click beetles will do the same things the click beetle in the story did or will they choose to do something different? Why?

4. Optional: Use a teaching clock to show morning, noon, evening and night times while children show their drawings to the group.

108

Tech Tie-In:

◆ Play this highly recommended computer game available as an individual CD or as one of the activities on Millie's Math House by Edmark. Children can practice number recognition, counting, and following directions as they take turns adding body parts to a silly bug.

> *Build a Math Bug*. 1999. Win/Mac. Edmark. (6727 185th Ave. NE. Redmond, WA 98073)

> *Millie's Math House*. 1995. Win/Mac. Edmark. (6727 185th Ave. NE. Redmond, WA 98073)

Time-of-Day Reproducible

Come On, Rain!

JUV
HS87c

by Karen Hesse

Hesse, Karen, *Come On, Rain!* Scholastic, 1999, 32 pp., 0-590-33125-6

Everyone is waiting for the rain. While Tess's Mamma tends the wilted plants in her little patch of garden, Tess watches the sky. She cleverly gets her mother to let her wear her bathing suit and join her friends. They wait expectantly in the hot alleyway.

When the rain finally comes, the girls make so much noise that their mothers all come out on their stoops to see what's going on. Then, one after another, all the mothers throw off shoes and stockings and join their daughters in a riotous dance through the rain.

◆ Skills Table ◆

Activity	Time	Location	Subjects	Skills	Standards
Hats Off!	P: 5 min. A: 15 min.	C, H, L	Language Arts Theatre Math	Interpret poetry; rhyming Using props to dramatize Transformations & symmetry	NCTE 3 MENC-T6 NCTM 3
Dressed for the Weather	P: 25 min. A: 15 min.	C, H, L	Science Math Language Arts Technology	Predicting weather Patterns; probability Exchange information through speech Collect information; problem solving	NAS- D NCTM 2, 5 NCTE 12 ISTE 5,6

P: Approximate Preparation Time   **A:** Approximate Activity Time   **C:** Classroom Activity
H: Home Activity   **L:** Library Activity

Hats Off!

Folded newspaper illustrates this simple rhyme that children recite as they make their own paper hats.

Supplies:

◆ One double-page spread of black and white newspaper for each child

◆ Stapler

Preparation:

◆ Practice the paper folding directions before demonstrating to the group.

Discussion:

Write the poem on the board:

Rainfall

Rain falls from the cloudy sky,

Rain falls on the mountain high.

Rain falls on boats upon the sea,

Rain falls down on top of me!

Recite the poem before asking:

Do you ever play outside in the rain?

What kinds of clothing do you wear?

Do you use an umbrella to keep you dry?

What special clothing do people wear to stay dry in the rain? (raincoat, rain boots, rain hat)

Activity:

1. Say the rhyme while folding the newspaper to form a mountain, a boat and finally, a rain hat.

2. Give each child a double-page spread of newspaper. Show them how to fold the newspaper as they say the rhyme.

3. Encourage children to share the "story rhyme" with their families.

Paper Folding Directions

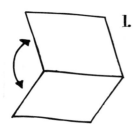

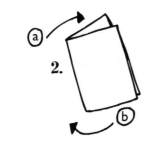

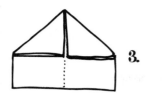

1. Begin with the double-page spread folded (as it comes in the newspaper). Fold it in half crosswise on the crease that already exists.

2. Fold the two sides together lengthwise and then open them back up.

3. Fold the top left and right corners to the center crease to make a pointed mountain shape.

4. Fold up the bottom edge on one side of the newspaper until it touches the base of the triangles. Do the same thing on the other side. Move the "boat" shape up and down on pretend waves.

5. Fold up both bottom edges again and staple through all layers on the far left and right sides of the "brim" of the hat. Staple as close to the edge as possible to make the hat as large as possible. Put the hat on so the widest parts of the hat are facing to the front and back, like a rain hat. Remove the hat to get a soaking just like the girls and their mothers enjoyed in *Come On, Rain!*

Variation:

Instead of having children make their own hats, you can simply make a hat to illustrate the rhyme.

Dressed for the Weather

Children decide how to dress for the weather by reading symbols on a weather map.

Supplies:

- ◆ Two copies of the weather symbol cards reproducible
- ◆ One copy of the boy and girl figures with clothing reproducible
- ◆ Flannel board
- ◆ ½ yard of medium weight fabric interfacing (available wherever fabrics are sold)
- ◆ Glue stick
- ◆ Scissors
- ◆ Fine point markers

Preparation:

- ◆ Cut apart one copy of the weather symbol reproducible. Use the other to introduce the symbols.
- ◆ Place interfacing over the boy, girl, and clothing. Trace and cut out patterns. Color with markers.
- ◆ Turn the symbol cards upside down and place them with the clothing by the flannel board.
- ◆ Place the boy and girl figures on the flannel board.

Discussion:

Show children the page of weather symbols.

> Weather maps have special symbols. Does the snow symbol look like snow?
> Does the rain symbol look like rain?
> What about... (Continue with the remaining symbols).

Explain that these symbols are used on television to show the weather on a weather map.

> What is the difference between the rain symbol and the heavy rain symbol?
> What is the difference between the heavy snow symbol and the snow symbol?
> Do all kinds of weather require special clothing? (No—fog does not.)

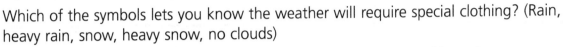

Which of the symbols lets you know the weather will require special clothing? (Rain, heavy rain, snow, heavy snow, no clouds)

What would you wear in heavy rain? (umbrella, rain poncho, and boots)

What would you wear in heavy snow? (coat, hat, and mittens)

Activity:

1. Have children take turns selecting a weather symbol card, a boy or girl figure, and clothing appropriate for the weather shown on the card.

2. Choices will depend on what is most commonly worn in your area, but more protective clothing should be chosen for heavy rain and heavy snow.

3. Play until everyone has had a turn.

Variation:

1. Make two copies of the weather symbol reproducible.

2. Use a correction pen to eliminate the words from one copy and cut apart.

3. Use the uncut reproducible with the words to introduce the activity.

4. Play as directed above.

Tech Tie-In:

◆ Web site: http://www.wunderground.com

 View weather maps based on various characteristics. Select the map type, city, and state.

◆ Listen to and learn songs about why the weather changes with *Weather*. Kim Mitzo Thompson and Karen Mitzo Hildenbrand, 1999. Twin Sister Productions, Inc. (2680 West Market St., Akron, OH 44333). An activity book is also available.

◆ Tune into a local weather forecast on television. Have children identify symbols on the television map and decide how to dress based on the forecast.

Weather Symbol Cards Reproducible

Rain	**Heavy Rain**
No Clouds	**Fog**
Snow	**Heavy Snow**

Boy, Girl, and Clothing Patterns

Good Night, Good Knight
by Shelley Moore Thomas

JUV
T462g

**Thomas, Shelley Moore, *Good Night, Good Knight*.
Dutton, 2000, 47 pp., 0-525-46326-7**

The three little dragons are lonely. No one but a good knight can help them get a good night's sleep. When he hears the loud roars of the dragons in their cave, the good knight investigates. After several trips to the cave, repeated glasses of water, bedtime stories, and songs, the knight is exasperated. What else could the dragons want? Goodnight kisses, of course!

Plan this activity for a large uncluttered area and be prepared for lots of requests for books about knights, dragons, and castles.

◆ Skills Table ◆

Activity	Time	Location	Subjects	Skills	Standards
To the Rescue	P: 20 min. A: 10–15 min.	C, L	Language Arts PE	Spelling; homophones Movement forms; responsibility; respect	NCTE 3, 6 NASPE 1, 5, 6
Dragon Kisses	P: 10 min. A: 15–20 min.	C, H, L	Language Arts Art Technology	Communicate through written language; rhyme words Choose subject matter Develop positive attitudes toward technology	NCTE 4, 6 MENC-A 3 ISTE 2

P: Approximate Preparation Time   **A:** Approximate Activity Time   **C:** Classroom Activity
H: Home Activity   **L:** Library Activity

Good Night, Good Knight by Shelly Moore Thomas

To the Rescue

Armor-clad knights race to spell the homophones, knight and night.

Supplies:

- Four disposable aluminum cake pans
- Two 16" pieces of yarn: red and blue
- Red and blue craft foam
- Hole punch
- Black marker
- One copy each of crest, knight, stars, and moon reproducibles

- Eleven 3" x 5" index cards
- Scissors
- Glue gun
- Hot glue
- Two chairs

Preparation:

- Place the crest pattern over the red foam to cut one crest shape. Repeat with blue foam.
- Hot glue the red crest to the bottom of one pan and the blue crest to the bottom of another pan.
- To make the "shoulder straps" for the armor, punch two holes in the top edges of all four pans, about one inch from where the top edge begins to curve.
- Use red yarn to tie the pan with the red crest to an unmarked pan. Repeat with blue yarn for the other set.
- Use a marker to print one letter of the words "knight" and "night" on each index card.
- Place two chairs at one end of the playing area. Place the "Knight" picture and lettered cards on one chair. Place two "Night" pictures and lettered cards on the other chair. (Two "night" pictures are used because knight has one more letter than night.)

Discussion:

Hold up the "knight" and "night" pictures. Say and spell each word aloud.

> What do you notice about the words "knight" and "night"?
>
> Both words sound alike, but do they have the same meaning?
>
> Are they spelled the same?

119

Even though the words sound alike, they have different meanings and are spelled differently. These words are called homophones.

Tell the children they will be playing a spelling relay race where they will leave the *castle* to "rescue" pictures and letters from the *cave*. The letters spell the two homophones, "knight" and "night."

Activity:

1. Divide children into a red team and a blue team. (If there is an uneven number of children, select players to run the relay twice. If there are more than 14 players total, some players will run the relay without picking up a letter.)

2. Line up teams at one end of the playing area *(the castle)* opposite the two chairs *(the cave).*

3. Designate one area for children to remove their armor to avoid "knights" from hitting their teammates.

4. Each knight must put on the armor (with the crest on the front) and rescue a picture or letter in the correct order to spell "Knight" and "Night." (Pictures should be picked up first. The "Night" team will pick up two pictures.)

5. Each knight must follow these directions: *(Demonstrate as you recite the rules.)*

   ◆ Say, "To the rescue!"
   ◆ Gallop to the other end of the room.
   ◆ Gallop around the chair.
   ◆ Pick up the correct picture or letter.
   ◆ Gallop back to the team.
   ◆ Place his/her picture or letter face up on the floor next to the team.
   ◆ Hand off the armor to the next knight in line.
   ◆ Repeat until the word is illustrated and spelled.

6. The winning team must finish first and spell their word correctly. Knights must start over if they take the wrong letter, run rather than gallop, forget to say, "To the rescue!", forget to go around the chair, or put armor on backward (crest on the back).

Tech Tie-In:

◆ Web site www.yourchildlearns.com/heraldry offers free, downloadable software for children to create their own heraldic design. Instructions provided.

Crest Pattern

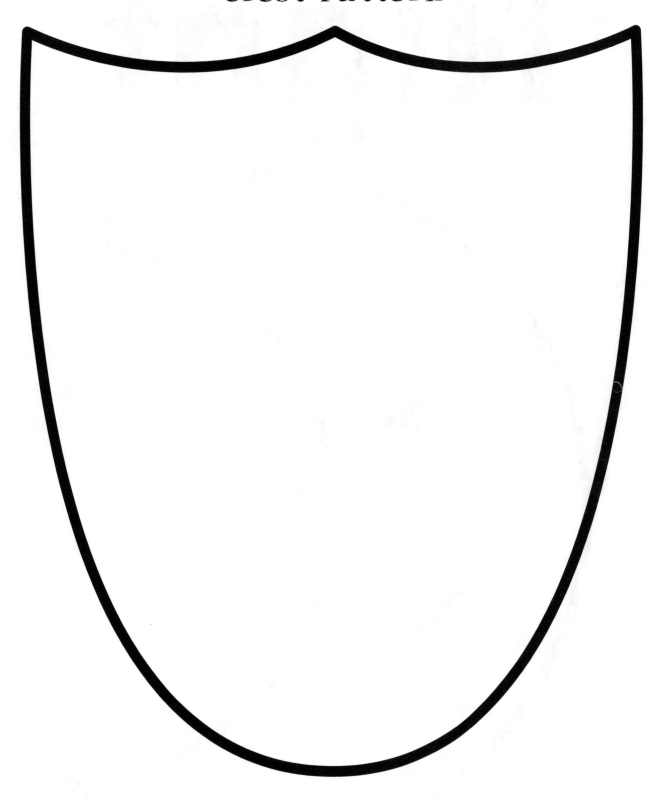

121

Night

122

Night

Knight

Dragon Kisses

Could anything be worse than kissing a dragon? Let children finish the poem, "I'd Rather Kiss a Dragon," by filling in the blanks with things they dislike.

Supplies:

◆ One "I'd Rather Kiss a Dragon" poem for each child

◆ Pencils and crayons

Discussion:

(Ask after reading the book to the children.)

What do you think it would be like to kiss a dragon?

What would be worse than kissing a dragon?

What do you dislike doing?

Would you rather kiss a dragon or do something else you dislike?

Why?

Activity:

1. Read the poem, inserting some of the disliked activities children mentioned.

2. Give each child a copy of the poem. Help them fill in the blanks with phrases that describe something they dislike.

3. Have them illustrate the poem by drawing a picture of themselves kissing a dragon or doing one of the things they dislike.

4. Display the finished poems on a bulletin board with the heading, "Dragon Kisses." Add a list of books about dragons, knights, and castles available in the library.

Tech Tie-In:

◆ Listen to this theme-based CD while completing the Dragon Kisses poem. Before they're finished, the children will be singing along:

Castles, Knights & Unicorns. Ronno, 2001. Kimbo Educational (P.O. Box 477, Long Branch, NJ 07740)

I'd Rather Kiss a Dragon

I'd rather kiss a dragon
On its scaly cheek

than _____
Any day of the week.

Their kisses may be scratchy
And their breath could scorch a tree,
But it's better

than _____
I'm sure you will agree.

There aren't too many dragons
So I think it's safe to say,
I'd rather kiss a dragon

Than _____
Any day!

Growing Frogs
by Vivian French

French, Vivian, *Growing Frogs*. Candlewick Press, 2000, 30 pp., 0-7636-0317-1

After a fanciful bedtime story about a frog that grows bigger and bigger, a little girl and her mother visit a local pond. There they collect frog eggs, which they bring home to observe. Bold, colorful paintings show the development of frog eggs as they change into tadpoles and finally, baby frogs. An early morning rain at the end of the story finds mother and daughter back at the pond surrounded by tiny, jumping frogs that they have wisely released back into their natural habitat.

This entertaining story is packed with facts. Additional information about the mating and growth of frogs is given in small type throughout the book for those children wanting more detail.

◆ Skills Table ◆

Activity	Time	Location	Subjects	Skills	Standards
The Perfect Place	P: 25 min. A: 10 min.	C, H, L	Science Math Language Arts	Frog life cycle and habitat Patterns; shapes; problem solving Predicting events in a story	NAS- C NCTM 2, 3, 6 NCTE 3

P: Approximate Preparation Time   **A:** Approximate Activity Time   **C:** Classroom Activity
H: Home Activity   **L:** Library Activity

The Perfect Place

Do this activity after reading the story *Growing Frogs* by Vivian French. Children can share their knowledge of frogs while participating in a story about a little girl's encounter with the frog world.

Supplies:

◆ Frog, tadpole, eye and grass patterns

◆ Green and black felt; one square of each

◆ Flannel board

◆ Construction paper: green and white

◆ Scissors

◆ Stapler

◆ Black fine point permanent marker

◆ Glue stick

◆ White chalk

◆ Small plastic bucket with handle

Preparation:

◆ Using the patterns, cut the frog from green felt, the tadpoles from black felt, the eyes from white construction paper and grass from green construction paper.

◆ Use chalk to copy the details of the frog's legs on the felt frog. Trace the chalk outline with the black marker. Brush away chalk residue.

◆ Use the black marker to make the eye pupils. Glue a small piece of black felt to the back of each eye.

◆ Glue small pieces of black felt to the back of the grass.

◆ Place the frog on the flannel board. Cover the bottom of the frog with the grass so that the legs are disguised and the frog looks like a green "pond." The eyes and tadpoles are added as the story is read.

Activity:

Read "The Perfect Place" to the group. (Instructions are in parentheses and should not be read aloud.)

Growing Frogs by Vivian French

The Perfect Place

I'm going to ask you to help me tell a story about a little girl who wanted a pet frog. During the story the little girl says, "Ooooo, Eeeee, THAT'S no place for a frog to be!" (Put your hands on either side of your face and grimace as you say the lines. Use this cue each time the line is spoken.)

The little girl says this a lot. So whenever I do this (put your hands on either side of your face and grimace), I want you to say, "Ooooo, Eeeee, THAT'S no place for a frog to be!" Let's practice.

Once there was a little girl who wanted a frog for a pet. Her mother told her she could find one at the pond near her house. So the little girl went to the pond to look for a frog, but when she saw the pond she said, (cue) "Ooooo, Eeeee, THAT'S no place for a frog to be!"

You see, the pond was covered in green slime and there were weeds growing around the edge (point to the green "pond" on the flannel board). Of course, the little girl didn't know that was JUST the place for a frog to be. But YOU know.

The little girl saw some blobs with black dots in them floating on the pond. (Place the eyes on the frog.) They looked disgusting! The little girl said (cue), "Ooooo, Eeeee, THAT'S no place for a frog to be!" But YOU know that's JUST the place for a frog to be, because you know the blobs were really . . . (pause for answer) frog eggs.

The little girl looked into the green water of the pond and she saw some black wiggly things swimming very fast. (Place the tadpoles head to head so they make a smile in the appropriate spot for the frog's mouth.) They looked disgusting! The little girl said, (cue) "Ooooo, Eeeee, THAT'S no place for a frog to be!" But YOU know that's JUST the place for a frog to be, because you know the black, wiggly things were really . . . (pause for answer) tadpoles.

The little girl walked to the other side of the pond where the tall weeds grew. She said, "THAT looks like the spot where a frog might be."

What do you think? (Pause for answer)

Well, let's see. (Pull away grass so the children can see the outline of the frog.)

YES! And the little girl said, "Ooooo, Eeeee, that's JUST the place for a frog to be!" So she put him in her bucket (put frog in bucket) . . . and took him home for her mother to see. She was so happy she sang all the way home.

(If you wish, use the song, "I'm Bringing Home a Baby Bumblebee" to make up your own song about a baby frog.)

Frog, Tadpole, Eyes, and Grass Patterns

Jamela's Dress

JUV
DIS3j

by Niki Daly

Daly, Niki, *Jamela's Dress*. Farrar, Straus & Giroux, 1999, 31 pp., 0-374-33667-9

Jamela admires the material her mother bought to make herself a dress for Thema's wedding. It is the most beautiful material she has ever seen. Instead of keeping the dog away from the material as it dries on the clothesline, Jamela wraps herself in it and marches through town.

What a commotion Jamela causes! Children, chickens, dogs and a bicycle all get mixed up with her mother's beautiful material. In the end, generosity and understanding create a way for Jamela and her mother to both have new dresses for the wedding. Although this story is set in Africa, it could take place anywhere.

◆ Skills Table ◆

Activity	Time	Location	Subjects	Skills	Standards
Far Across the Ocean	P: 30 min. A: Several days research	C, H, L	Geography Art Info. Literacy Technology Language Arts	People and places; perceptions Cultural understanding Work in groups to use information Create product through research Understand cultures	NGS 4, 6 MENC- A 4 ALA 1, 3, 9 ISTE 2, 3, 4, 5 NCTE 1
Window Shopping	P: 15 min. A: 20 min.	C, H, L	Art Geography Math	Cultural understanding People & places Patterns; symmetry	MENC-A4 NGS 4 NCTM 2, 3

P: Approximate Preparation Time   **A:** Approximate Activity Time   **C:** Classroom Activity
H: Home Activity   **L:** Library Activity

Jamela's Dress by Niki Daly

Far Across the Ocean

This collaborative research activity will help children discover another country. Through books, magazines and the Internet, they will create artwork to illustrate a poem of harmony. Be sure to schedule several research sessions for the children.

Supplies:

- Current non-fiction books about a pre-selected country

- Transparency and overhead projector

- One transparency of "Far Across the Ocean" poem

- Computer with Internet capability

- Optional: One copy of "Far Across the Ocean" reproducible for each child

- One large sheet of art paper for each child

- One sheet of lined drawing paper for each child

- Copy paper

- Photographs of domestic life in other countries

- Pencils and crayons

- Optional: Multimedia software (Power Point® or HyperStudio®)

Preparation:

- Copy "Far Across the Ocean" onto a transparency for use on the overhead projector.

- Bookmark Web sites to use when researching a country as indicated in the Tech Tie-In section.

- Select media materials for the pre-selected country that will provide at least one fact for each of these topics: word or phrase, flag, animal, holiday, shape of country, and people.

Discussion:

(Ask after reading the book to the children.)

Show illustrations from the book as you ask these questions:

> How is Jamela's clothing like yours?
> How is Jamela's clothing different?
> Is her house like yours?
> What is different about her house?

Show the illustration of Archie giving Jamela's mother the material. Point out the peaches on the shelves and what appears to be a Coca-Cola® sign on the Snak-Pak store.

> Does she eat the same foods that you eat?

Activity:

1. Show "Far Across the Ocean" on the overhead projector as you read the poem aloud.

2. Ask children to copy the poem "Far Across the Ocean" onto a piece of lined paper. (Or give each student a copy of the reproducible.) Turn the art paper with the long sides at the top and bottom. Glue the poem in the center of the paper.

3. Show the children several photographs of other countries. Ask them what they see that is like their own country and what is different.

4. Show the children a photograph of the country they will be researching.

5. Tell the children they will be learning about that country by finding information in books and on the Internet. Then they can illustrate their poems with images and drawings about the country.

6. Help children print the name of the country in large letters across the top of the art paper.

7. Show the children the pre-selected media sources, including the Internet.

8. Help the children find a word or phrase from the country.

9. Have them illustrate the word or phrase on the border of their poem.

10. Repeat for flag, animal, holiday, shape of country, and people.

11. Display the finished projects on a bulletin board under the heading, "We all go out to play."

12. Optional: Collect the images to create a computer slide show.

Tech Tie-In:

◆ Web site: http://ipl.si.umich.edu/div/kidspace/cquest/

Children can learn about Jamela's world by visiting this Web site. Olivia Owl and Parsifal Penguin give the children a tour of different countries. Begin by visiting Africa, then encourage children to explore the information about other countries.

◆ Web site: http://www.countryreports.org

Children can learn important facts about countries, view their flags, listen to their national anthem and even view the lyrics in English or the language of that particular country.

◆ Web site: www.pics4learning.com

This Web site contains copyright-friendly images for use by teachers and students in an educational setting. You can browse by topic and link to countries and flags.

Far Across the Ocean

Far across the ocean,

Far across the sea,

Live a boy and girl

A lot like you and me.

Our houses may be different,

Our food is not the same.

But each day when the sun comes out

We all go out to play.

134

Jamela's Dress by Niki Daly

Window Shopping

Children choose the material to put in the textile store window for the big sale. Like Mnandi's Textile Shop, the material the children select will have varied and colorful patterns.

Supplies:

◆ Copies of the Textile Shop reproducible   ◆ Crayons and pencils

Preparation:

◆ Make one copy of the reproducible for each child plus two for samples.

◆ Complete one sample with pencil as described in activity. Do not color it. Complete a second sample in color.

Discussion:

(Ask after reading the book to the children.)

Show children the picture of Mnandi's Textile Shop.

> What does the store have the most of? What do you think the word textile means?
>
> What is another name for material or textile? (fabric)
>
> What different patterns do you see in Mnandi's Textile Shop?
>
> Do the patterns on all material repeat?
>
> How are these designs like the designs on our clothing?
>
> How are they different?

Activity:

1. Show the children the Textile Shop handout. Look at each pattern in detail and discuss how the pattern in each piece of material repeats.

2. Give each child a copy of the Textile Shop handout. Show them your pencil sample.

3. Have children choose four fabric patterns they would like in their store windows. Use a pencil to copy one pattern in each store window. Fill up the windows completely with the designs.

4. Show the children the color sample. Have them color the four pieces of material in the boxes at the bottom of the page. Then have them color the four pieces of material they drew in the store windows. Remind children that the patterns and colors should be the same.

135

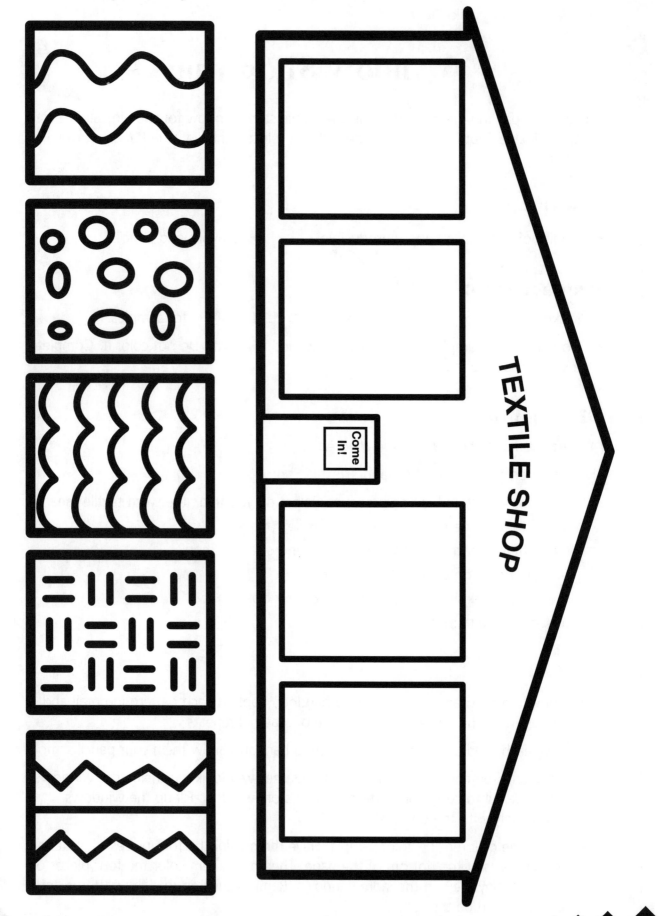

TEXTILE SHOP

Come In!

Jingle Dancer
by Cynthia Leitich Smith

JUV
S644j

Smith, Cynthia Leitich, *Jingle Dancer*. Morrow Junior Books, 2000, 32 pp., 0-688-16242-8

Follow Jenna, a Native American girl from the Muscogee (Creek) Nation, as she makes her way around the neighborhood asking friends and relatives for jingles to complete her jingle dress.

The wonderful watercolor illustrations by Cornelius Van Wright and Ying-Hwa Hu show clearly that Native Americans today live much like boys and girls across the United States. Factual information about Jingle Dancing as well as a glossary can be found at the end of the book.

Jingles are hollow and do not have bells in them. The sound of the jingles is made from the jingles clinking together as the dancer moves. To recreate the sound of the jingles, "pretend" jingles are used in the "May I?" activity.

◆ Skills Table ◆

Activity	Time	Location	Subjects	Skills	Standards
May I?	P: 45 min. A: 20 min.	C, L	History Language Arts Theatre Technology	Native American life today Story recall Dramatics Information gathering	NCHS 1 NCTE 3 MENC- T2 ISTE 5
Fry Bread (Additional Activity)	P: none A: 10 min.	C, L	Math Health	Patterns of sounds Listening skills	NCTM 2 AAHE 5

P: Approximate Preparation Time   **A:** Approximate Activity Time   **C:** Classroom Activity
H: Home Activity   **L:** Library Activity

May I?

Children learn good manners as they act out the story of *Jingle Dancer* by Cynthia Leitich Smith.

Supplies:

- 16 foil mini muffin baking cups
- Ruler, scissors, glue stick, clear adhesive tape, package of crayons or markers
- 16 paper clips
- 16 small jingle bells
- Brown paper lunch bag
- Four plastic zipper bags
- Hot glue gun and hot glue
- One yard of lace trim with a loop design
- Jingle dancer pattern
- White poster board
- Wooden paint stick

Preparation:

Making jingles (Make 16):

- Flatten the foil baking cup and fold it in half.
- Open a paper clip into an "S" shape. Hook the smaller hook of the "S" through the loop in the top of the jingle bell. Pinch the paper clip together above the bell to secure it.
- Lay the paper clip and bell on top of the foil semi-circle. The center of the "S" should be even with the straight (top) edge of the semi-circle.
- Roll the foil tightly into a narrow cone shape around the paper clip. Pinch the top of the jingle around the paper clip to secure it. Tape if needed.
- Put four jingles in each plastic zipper bag.

Making jingle dancer:

- Copy both pieces of the jingle dancer pattern. Line up the two pieces and glue them to the poster board. Color the jingle dancer, laminate and cut out.
- Cut and hot glue three pieces of fabric trim to fit on the jingle dancer's skirt. Refer to the book illustrations for placement.
- Cut and glue trim for the top of the dress. The trim around the top of the dress will need to be "gathered" as you glue so that it follows the curve of the blouse.
- Hot glue the wooden paint stirring stick to the back of the jingle dancer for a handle.

138

Making the bag:

- Cut a 3" strip from the top of the lunch bag.

- Cut 2" slits thorough both layers to make a fringe for the bottom of the bag. Slide the fringed portion over the paper bag so that the bottom edge of the fringe is even with the bottom of the bag.

- Glue fringe to the bag. Use crayons or markers to draw a design similar to the one on Jenna's bag.

Activity:

1. Read *Jingle Dancer*, including the Author's Note and Glossary.

2. Choose four children to act out the story. You will play the role of the grandmother.

3. Give a jingle bag to each character except Jenna.

4. The child acting the part of Jenna should politely ask each of the other characters for jingles which she places in the paper bag.

5. Just as in the story, the ones lending the jingles will ask Jenna to dance for them.

6. As the grandmother, you will give her the last row of jingles and then "sew" all of the jingles on the jingle dancer's dress by hooking the paper clips through loops in the lace.

7. Ask the discussion questions as you hang the jingles.

8. When you finish, make the jingle dancer bounce step by holding the stick and moving the jingle dancer up and down.

Discussion:

How did Jenna honor the women who loaned her the jingles? (by dancing for them at the powwow when they were not able to)

Why is the number 4 emphasized in the story?

What is special about the jingle dance?

Fry Bread (Additional Activity):

Make fry bread from a Tech Tie-In recipe. Chant this rhyme with the children as you share the fry bread (hand gestures are in parentheses):

Mix it up. *(stir)*

Knead it well. *(knead)*

Pat it round. *(pat)*

Fry it. *(flip hands with palms together)*

Spread the butter. *(spread with knife)*

Add some honey. *(pour)*

Eat it up. *(bite)*

Try it! *(rub tummy)*

Tech Tie-In:

◆ www.cynthialeitichsmith.com/jingledancerlinks.htm

This Web site offers discussion questions and many curriculum links to *Jingle Dancer*. A fry bread recipe is included.

Children will learn about how the powwow began and how it has changed while watching national champions dance and listening to interviews with dancers, singers and tribal elders.

◆ This video is a National Educational Film and Video Award Winner:

Into the Circle. 1992. 58 min. Full Circle Communications.
(1131 S. College Ave., Tulsa, OK 74104)

Top Half of Jingle Dancer Pattern

Bottom Half of Jingle Dancer Pattern

Joseph Had a Little Overcoat

by Simms Taback

JUV
T112j

**Taback, Simms, *Joseph Had a Little Overcoat*.
Viking, 1999, 36 pp., 0-670-87855-3**

Joseph's overcoat is very old and worn. Not willing to discard it, he recycles it. First it becomes a jacket and, finally, a button when only a shred of useable fabric is left. One day he loses his button. Now he has nothing. Or does he?

In this newly illustrated version of a book Simms Taback previously wrote, Joseph finds you can always make something from nothing. Like his Caldecott Honor book, *There was an Old Lady Who Swallowed a Fly*, this book uses a die-cut format to give children glimpses of what is to come on the next page. It's easy to see why this book won the Caldecott Medal.

◆ Skills Table ◆

Activity	Time	Location	Subjects	Skills	Standards
Say Mazl-tov	P: 20 min. A: 20–25 min.	C, H, L	Language Arts Art Technology	Respect for diversity in language Art and cultures Collect information	NCTE 9 MENC- A4 ISTE 5
Joseph Had a Little Button, Additional Activity	P: none A: 10 min.	C, L	Health	Non-verbal communication	AAHE 5

P: Approximate Preparation Time   **A:** Approximate Activity Time   **C:** Classroom Activity
H: Home Activity   **L:** Library Activity

Say Mazl-tov

Children discover that congratulations in any language are always nice to give and receive as they make a Mazl-tov sampler to share.

Note that although there are alternate spellings of Mazl-tov, the spelling in *Joseph Had a Little Overcoat* by Simms Taback is the one that is used for this activity.

Supplies:

◆ Copy paper cut into 4" squares

◆ Four wooden craft sticks per child plus four extra

◆ Washable markers

◆ Glue gun and hot glue

◆ Additional Activity: one button

Preparation:

◆ Prepare a Mazl-tov sampler by following the directions below.

Discussion:

(Ask after reading the book to the children.)

Show the illustrations to the children.

   What country does Joseph live in? (Poland)

   How can you tell? (Look at envelopes addressed to him.)

There are many posters, pictures and needlework samplers on Joseph's walls. A needlework sampler is usually a proverb, or saying, that is sewn on cloth with pretty thread. Often there are pictures or designs sewn on the cloth as well.

   Are all of the samplers on Joseph's wall written in English? (No—the other languages are Hebrew and Yiddish.)

   Is the sampler with the word Mazl-tov written in English? (No—Hebrew)

   The word Mazl-tov means congratulations.

   What occasions can you think of when you congratulate someone?

Activity:

1. Show the sampler you made and examples from the book.

2. Give each child a 4" square of paper.

3. Using the markers, help the children print Mazl-tov in the center of the paper, then decorate with designs.

4. Remind children to leave room at the edges for the craft-stick frame.

5. Have children bring their sampler to you for framing.

6. Frame by gluing overlapping craft sticks to the border of the paper.

7. After the glue dries, children can draw a dotted line to represent stitching around the perimeter of the sampler.

8. Display the Mazl-tov samplers for all the visitors to the library.

Additional Activity:

Play "Joseph Had a Little Button," following the format of "Button, Button."

Tech Tie-In:

◆ http://www.ibiblio.org/yiddish/school.html/

   Children can click on "Kindergarten" for a language adventure. Both "Wordmatch" and "Find a Match for Each Word" match written Yiddish words with pictures. "Wordmatch" has several languages to choose from, as well as an audio option for word pronunciation.

◆ Watch the video of *Joseph Had a Little Overcoat* and compare it to the book. *Joseph Had a Little Overcoat*. 2001. 10 minutes. Includes teachers guide. Weston Woods. (265 Post Road West, Westport, CT 06880)

Mike Mulligan and His Steam Shovel
by Virginia Lee Burton

JUV
B974m

Burton, Virginia Lee, *Mike Mulligan and His Steam Shovel*.
Houghton Mifflin, 1967, 44 pp., 0-395-16961-5

This book was first published in 1939, yet Mike Mulligan's belief in himself and his steam shovel, Mary Anne, continues to be a heart-warming tale sure to inspire children as well as adults. The comical illustrations are detailed enough to encourage discussions about how things have changed over the years, and to imagine how things might be in the future.

◆ Skills Table ◆

Activity	Time	Location	Subjects	Skills	Standards
Dig It!	P: 40 min. A: 10–20 min.	C, L	Language Arts Theatre Health Technology	Understand human experience; story recall Act out roles Listening skills Enhanced learning & creativity	NCTE 2, 3 MENC- T2 AAHE 5 ISTE 3
My Moon Machine	P: 10 min. A: 25–30 min. minimum	C, H, L	History Geography Science Art Info. Literacy Technology	Compare past and present Human impact on environment Earth & space; technological design Influence of scientific information on design Evaluate and use information creatively Evaluate & select new information resources	NCHS 2 NGS 14 NAS- D, E MENC- A6 ALA 2, 3 ISTE 5

P: Approximate Preparation Time   **A:** Approximate Activity Time   **C:** Classroom Activity
H: Home Activity   **L:** Library Activity

Dig It!

Through creative props, children can retell the story of *Mike Mulligan and His Steam Shovel*.

Supplies:

- One empty cube-shaped tissue box; brown preferred
- One wooden craft stick
- Glue gun and hot glue
- Stapler
- Ruler
- Crayons

- Construction paper: two pieces of brown; one yellow; one blue
- One yellow plastic soda bottle lid
- One copy of the reproducible
- Scissors
- Glue

Preparation:

- Color and cut out both steam shovels and the city hall.

- Glue the steam shovels back to back with the wooden craft stick sandwiched between them to make a puppet.

- Using the circle pattern, cut three circles from yellow construction paper. Staple two of the circles together in the center. Glue the third circle over the other two circles to cover up the smooth side of the staple.

- Cut out the bottom of the tissue box, approximately ½" from the edge. Leave the box upside down.

- Cut two box-size pieces of brown construction paper and glue to opposite sides of the box.

- Cut one blue and one brown piece of construction paper the same width as the other two sides of the box, but twice the height. Fold the brown paper in half, with the short sides together. Open the paper and glue the city hall to the top half. Glue the bottom half of the paper to the front side of the box. City hall should flap over the top of the box.

- Trace the arch pattern in the top half of the blue construction paper. Carefully cut out the groove. Cut as smoothly as possible, with no jagged edges.

- Glue the blue paper to the back of the box, so the arch extends above the box.

- Slide the sun into the groove so the circle without the staple showing is to the front of the groove.

◆ Make a handle to pull the sun by gluing the bottle cap upside down to the back circle. Slide the sun around the arch. If it does not move smoothly, use an emery board to smooth off any rough edges in the groove.

Discussion:

(As you read the book to the children, pause after Mike completes the cellar.)

Do you see a problem?

Can you think of any ways to get Mike and Mary Anne out of the hole they dug?

Finish reading the book.

Why did Henry B. Swap smile in a mean way?

Why did Henry B. Swap smile in a nicer way at the end of the story?

What kinds of stories do you think Mike Mulligan told in the cellar of the new town hall?

Activity:

1. Assign a part from the book for each child to retell or act out. Select one child to pull the sun across the sky.

2. While manipulating the steam shovel puppet, retell the story by referring to the book illustrations as you ask, "What happened next?"

3. Lower the puppet slightly as Mike digs deeper, until it is no longer visible after the fourth corner is dug.

4. At the point in the story where it is decided to build the town hall over Mike and Mary Anne, raise and hold the brown piece of paper so the town hall is visible. Then continue acting out the story as it was written.

Tech Tie-In:

◆ Children can build a steam shovel, move Mary Anne through a maze using their map skills, or play a memory game on this software:

Mike Mulligan and His Steam Shovel. 1996. WIN/MAC. Houghton Mifflin Interactive/Sunburst Technology. (1900 S. Batavia Ave., Geneva, 60134)

◆ Have children watch the musical version of *Mike Mulligan and His Steam Shovel* and decide how the music complements the story. Use as a springboard to think of other books that would make good musicals. *Mike Mulligan and his Steam Shovel Video recording: The Musical.* 1991. 30 min. Includes study guide. Ambrose Video Publication, Inc. (145 W. 45th St., Suite 1115, New York, NY 10036)

Steam Shovel, City Hall, Circle, and Arch

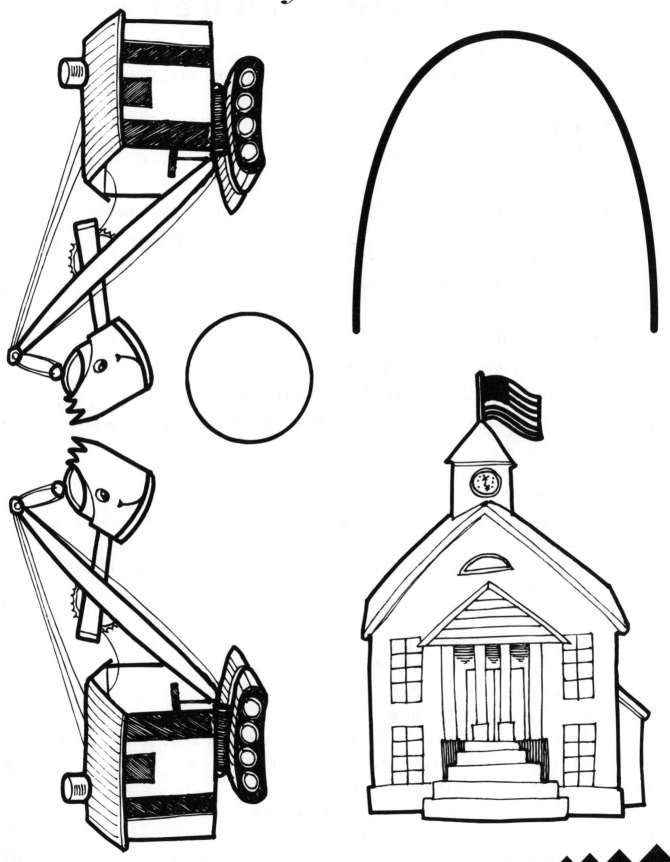

Mike Mulligan and His Steam Shovel by Virginia Lee Burton

My Moon Machine

Children can leap into the 21st century by traveling to the moon to imagine what kinds of equipment and machinery might be used at a future building site.

Supplies:

- ◆ My Moon Machine reproducible
- ◆ Crayons
- ◆ Several photographs from the 1930s showing cars, clothing and machinery
- ◆ Encyclopedias or other nonfiction books with pictures of astronauts and the lunar rover
- ◆ Computer with Internet connection

Preparation:

- ◆ Copy one reproducible for each child.
- ◆ Bookmark the Web sites if they will be viewed by the children.
- ◆ As an alternative, print the photographs from the Web sites to be used with the activity.

Discussion:

When was *Mike Mulligan and His Steam Shovel* written? (Look at the copyright date with children.)

How many years ago was that? (Count up by tens and then ones from 1939 to the present year.)

Show the photographs from the 1930s.

What kinds of clothing are people wearing?

How are these clothes different from what we wear today?

What else is different about these pictures?

How do you think the future will look?

What would Mike Mulligan look like if he was a construction worker on the moon?

What kind of job would you have on the moon?

What kind of clothing might you wear?

What kind of machinery and tools do you think you would use?

Activity:

1. Use the Web sites from the Tech Tie-In as well as encyclopedias and non-fiction books to view pictures of astronauts, the lunar rover, and lunar landing probe.

2. Have the children view the Web sites or show them the printed pages. Be sure to read the general information about the moon from the Level 1 area of the StarChild Web site.

3. Give each child a copy of the reproducible.

4. Ask the children to draw pictures of themselves and their machine constructing the first building on the moon. Remind them to make the moon environment as accurate as possible.

5. Display the finished pictures under the heading "Building the Future."

Tech Tie-In:

◆ http://StarChild.gsfc.nasa.gov

All sites are part of NASA's StarChild Web site. The address for the Web site is case sensitive and must be typed with a capital letter "S" and a capital letter "C."

Select "Search StarChild." Type moon in the blank.

Select from Level 1: Moon information.

Select from General Information:
Surveyor 3 on the surface of the moon
Apollo 15 Lunar Rover
Buzz Aldrin on the moon (Apollo 11)
Planting the American flag on the moon (Apollo 11)
Spacesuits for spacewalking.

My Moon Machine Reproducible

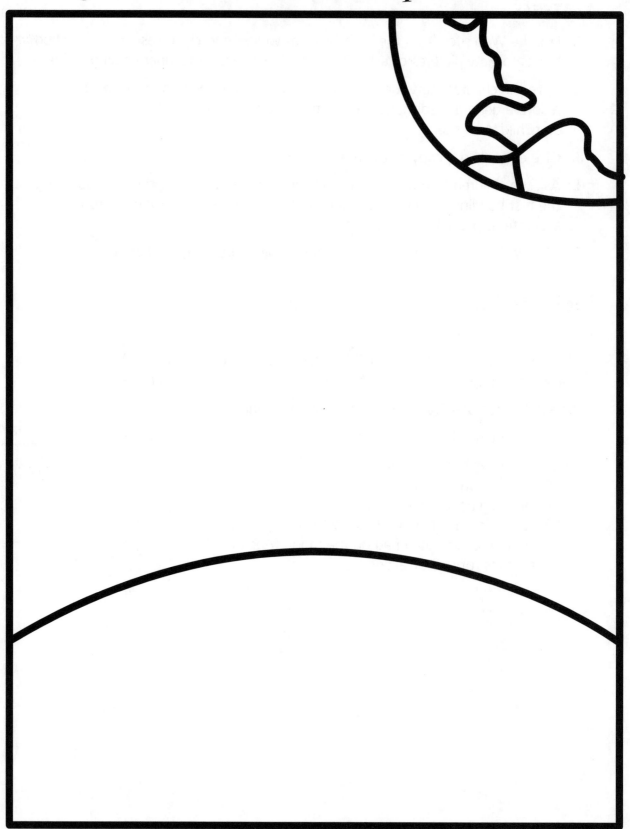

My Very Own Room

by Amada Irma Perez

Perez, Amada Irma, *My Very Own Room*. Children's Book Press, 2000, 32 pp., 0-89239-164-2

Sharing a bedroom with five brothers isn't easy. The little girl in this story longs for a space of her own, but that can be hard to find. She shares a small two-bedroom home not only with her brothers and parents, but sometimes with visiting relatives from Mexico as well. But with imagination and hard work, the little girl and her family find a space she can call her own.

This bilingual story is based on the author's very own family. Illustrated in brilliant colors, the story captures a family joining together to fulfill a little girl's wish.

◆ Skills Table ◆

Activity	Time	Location	Subjects	Skills	Standards
The Size of It: Measuring & Mapping	P: 15 min. A: 20–25 min.	C, H, L	Geography Math Language Arts	Map reading Measurements Cultural understanding	NGS 1 NCTM 4 NCTE 1
Presto Change-O	P: 45 min. A: 10–15 min.	C, H, L	Language Arts Math History	Cultural understanding; story recall Measurements; problem solving Immigration	NCTE 1, 3 NCTM 4, 6 NCHS 5

P: Approximate Preparation Time   **A:** Approximate Activity Time   **C:** Classroom Activity
H: Home Activity   **L:** Library Activity

The Size of It: Measuring

Using yellow yarn and the length of their own bodies, children can measure the size of the little girl's room.

Supplies:

◆ One skein of yellow yarn

◆ Masking tape

◆ Scissors

Preparation:

◆ None

Discussion:

(Ask after reading the book to the children.)

Was the little girl's room very big?

Was it bigger or smaller than your room?

Why did the little girl measure her room with the yarn?

How did she know if her uncle's bed would fit in her room?

Pull out a short piece of yarn from the skein.

Is this about how long the little girl's room was?

Do I need to make the yarn longer or shorter?

Was her room much longer than her bed?

Activity:

1. Reread the part of the story where the bed is eased into the room.

2. Ask one child to pull out a piece of yarn that is about as long as a bed.

3. Ask another child to lay down on the floor to help decide the bed's length.

4. Ask children to decide the length of the room and cut yarn to represent the length. Tape it to the floor.

5. As another child pulls out a piece of yarn as wide as the bed, ask:

   How much wider was the little girl's room?

   Was it just barely wide enough for the bed and a crate for a bedside table?

6. Cut the yarn to equal the approximate width of the little girl's room. Tape the yarn on the floor so it is perpendicular to and touches the end of the first piece of yarn.

7. Cut another piece of yarn the same length as the first piece to show the length of the curtain side of the room. Tape it on the floor to create the curtain wall.

8. Cut the last piece of yarn to connect the curtain wall with the back wall.

9. Let children take turns standing in the little girl's room to see if it is bigger or smaller than their room at home.

The Size of It: Mapping

Children create a bird's eye view as they map out the little girl's room.

Supplies:

◆ White paper   ◆ Pencils

Preparation:

Draw a bird's eye view map of the little girl's room:

1. Draw a rectangle to represent the little girl's bed and a smaller rectangle to represent the pillow on the bed.

2. Draw a square next to the bed to represent the crate and a circle on the crate for the lamp.

3. Draw six small rectangles on the bed to represent six library books.

4. Draw a large rectangle to represent the perimeter of the room.

5. Create a small map key in the lower right corner of the paper. The key should include a small drawing of the table, lamp and book with each one labeled.

Activity:

1. Show the children the map and explain that this is a bird's eye view of the little girl's room. This shows how things look from above.

2. Point out the map key. Explain that the key helps identify things not labeled on a map.

3. Ask the children to find the items in the room that are labeled. (Bed and pillow)

4. Ask the children to use the key to find the unlabeled items. (Lamp, books, and table)

5. Give each child a piece of white paper. Tell them they will make a map of their own bedroom.

6. Following the map of the little girl's room, have them draw and label their bed and pillow.

7. Have them draw three more objects from their bedroom and make a key to identify these objects.

8. Have them enclose the room with a perimeter.

9. Display the drawings under the heading "My Very Own Room."

156

Presto Change-O

Children can recall the events of *My Very Own Room* by recreating a miniature set design of the little girl's room.

Supplies:

◆ One yard of yellow yarn

◆ Construction paper: pink and green

◆ White copy paper

◆ Twelve craft sticks

◆ One copy of each reproducible

◆ Scissors

◆ Glue gun and hot glue

◆ Glue stick

Preparation:

◆ Cut two 12" pieces and two 6" pieces of yellow yarn to serve as a rectangular replica of the little girl's room. Tape to a flat surface to create a stage with access from all four sides.

◆ Color the reproducibles of the furnishings to match those in the book as much as possible.

◆ Cut out the furnishings. Glue the lamp, two sets of books, and the wooden crate to pink construction paper and the other pictures to green construction paper. Then cut out the pictures, leaving a border of construction paper around each one.

◆ Glue a craft stick to the construction paper backing of each cutout so the handle is at the top. Children will use the handle to move props around the stage.

Discussion:

(Ask these questions after reading the book to the children and during the activity as the children identify and move each of the props in and around the set while they recall the events of the story. Prompt them as needed to recall events in order.)

Why did the little girl's aunt and uncle need the sewing machine and garden tools to make a better life for themselves in this country?

What colors of paint did the little girl and her brothers mix together to paint her room?

What color did they make by mixing the colors together?

What did Raul use to make a bedside table for her room?

What did the little girl buy for her room?

What did she use to buy it?

Would you rather buy something with money or with stamps?

Why?

After the little girl had the bed, the bedside table and the lamp in her room, she knew the most important thing was missing. What was it?

Why did she get six books from the library?

Activity:

1. Give each child a prop to place on the stage. Help them decide the order their props will appear and disappear based on the sequence of events in the book.

2. Show the illustration of the store room so children can decide which props should be included on the stage.

3. Have the children remove the store room props from the stage in sequence, with the paint cans removed last.

4. Have the children move the bedroom props onto the stage in sequence to create the little girl's room.

Tech Tie-In:

◆ http://www.littleexplorers.com/languages/Spanishdictionary.html

Let children browse this user-friendly English-Spanish pictorial dictionary to expand their bilingual vocabulary.

◆ Give children a tour of bilingual dictionaries, posters, tapes, and other bilingual media available in the library.

Silver Seeds

by Paul Paolilli and Dan Brewer

**Paolilli, Paul and Brewer, Dan, *Silver Seeds*.
Viking, 2001, 32 pp., 0-670-88941-5**

These acrostic nature poems motivate children to look at nature in a different way. Are trees really like hands reaching up to tickle the sky?

The poems are so well done you may not notice that the first letter of each line spells the name of the poem. The closer you look, the more you will see in this book that takes you from sunrise to sunset with beautifully painted illustrations that are the perfect complement to the text.

◆ Skills Table ◆

Activity	Time	Location	Subjects	Skills	Standards
Listen Up!	P: 30 min. A: 15–25 min.	C, L	Health Language Arts Technology	Listening skills Aesthetic appreciation; comprehension and interpretation Promote creativity	AAHE 5 NCTE 2, 3 ISTE 3
Additional Activity: Library Cheer!	P: 15 min. A: 20–25 min.	C	Language Arts	Appreciate acrostic poetry; write to communicate; critique, discuss, and create text	NCTE 3,5,6

P: Approximate Preparation Time   **A:** Approximate Activity Time   **C:** Classroom Activity
H: Home Activity   **L:** Library Activity

Listen Up!

Children discover the magic of acrostic poems about nature as they listen to the poems and match each poem's theme with a flannel board picture.

Supplies:

◆ *Silver Seeds* by Paul Paolilli and Dan Brewer

◆ Copy of each reproducible

◆ Crayons, scissors and glue stick

◆ For Tech Tie-In: Computer with Internet connection
                    Multimedia projector

◆ Flannel board

◆ One piece of light colored felt

◆ Five legal size envelopes

Preparation:

◆ Copy the reproducibles.

◆ Color, laminate and cut out the pictures.

◆ Glue two small pieces of felt to the back of each picture.

◆ Label five envelopes with the following:

    Geographical Features and Plants
    Day
    Night
    Animals
    Weather

◆ Sort pictures by subject and place in the corresponding envelope.

◆ For Tech Tie-In: Review and bookmark the Web site.
                    Set up the projector.

Activity:

(This activity should be done as you read the book to the children.)

1. Introduce children to the features of acrostic poems by reading the first poem, "Dawn." Show them the picture in the book.

2. Point out that the subject of the poem is written vertically, and that the subject of the poem starts with the same letter as the first word in the poem. Stress the letter sound of the first word when reading the poems.

3. Place the three pictures from the "Day" envelope on the flannel board. Have the children pick the picture that matches the poem you read.

4. Hold the book so the children cannot see the pictures, then read the "Sun" poem. Have the children pick the picture that matches the poem.

5. Remind the children that the letters for the poem's subject will be the first letter of each line in the poem.

6. As each picture is correctly matched, ask the children how they knew the answer. Verify by showing the children the poem in the book. Remove the picture from the board.

7. Continue to place all the pictures from one envelope on the flannel board at a time, read one poem, and have children take turns identifying the subject.

Discussion:

(Ask these questions after reading the book and doing the activity.)

What do you see when you hear the poems read?

Do the poems rhyme?

What descriptive words can you recall from the poems?

What poems compared two things?

Is all poetry about nature?

Variation:

◆ For more of a challenge, complete the activity directions for the first poem. Then pass out the remaining pictures. Read the poems one at a time, asking the child with the matching picture to place it on the board. Verify correct answers by showing the group the poem and its corresponding illustration in the book.

Tech Tie-In:

◆ www.geocities.com/Enchanted Forest/5165/pages/acrostic.html

Click on this Web site to view acrostic poems created by children of similar age groups.

Additional Activity: Library Cheer!

◆ Collaborate with teachers to incorporate an acrostic poem writing assignment in the classroom using the word LIBRARY.

Poem Illustrations

Poem Illustrations

Moon

Clouds

Stars

Rain

Night

Fog

Poem Illustrations

Bee

Butterfly

Hummingbird

Watermelon Day
by Kathi Appelt

Appelt, Kathi, *Watermelon Day*. H. Holt, 1994, 34 pp., 0-8050-2304-6

The little girl first notices the watermelon when it is hiding under its leaves. Even though it's still small, it's bigger than all the other watermelons. She and her Pappy agree it will be just right for a Watermelon Day. The anticipation as the little girl waits all summer for the watermelon to ripen, and then all during the Watermelon Day for it to cool down in the pond, will have mouths watering.

The story is carefully crafted, and the words paint pictures as vivid as the brilliantly colored paintings that reflect the anticipation and excitement of a perfect family get-together on Watermelon Day.

◆ Skills Table ◆

Activity	Time	Location	Subjects	Skills	Standards
A Taste of Summer	P: 25 min. A: 20 min. Optional Additional Classroom Time	C, H, L Optional Collaborative Classroom Activity	Language Arts Technology Info. Literacy	Similes; write, critique & discuss poetry; literacy; community participation Publish & interact with peers & others Pursue information relating to personal interests	NCTE 3, 5, 6, 11 ISTE 4 ALA 4
Busy Bee	P: 30 min. A: 10–15 min.	C, H, L	Science Language Arts Theatre	Life cycle-plants; organisms-environment & characteristics Gather & synthesize information Acting by assuming roles	NAS- C NCTE 7 MENC-T2

P: Approximate Preparation Time **A:** Approximate Activity Time **C:** Classroom Activity
H: Home Activity **L:** Library Activity

Watermelon Day by Kathi Appelt

A Taste of Summer

How would you describe a watermelon? Let watermelon candy melt in your mouth while you write descriptive phrases on giant watermelon seeds. Put them all together to make a group poem, then take the idea back to class and write individual poems on individual watermelon slices.

Supplies for Library Activity:

◆ One watermelon seed reproducible

◆ Poster board: one red and one green

◆ Three 9" x 13" mailing envelopes

◆ Clear adhesive shelf paper

◆ Masking tape

◆ Permanent marker

◆ White liquid correction pen

◆ Glue stick

◆ Scissors

◆ Stapler

◆ Optional: One piece of watermelon flavored candy for each child

Preparation for Library Activity:

◆ Trim the edges of the green poster board to make a large semicircle. Cut a slightly smaller semicircle from red poster board.

◆ Make the watermelon slice by gluing the red piece to the green.

Watermelon
As cold as
As heavy as
As sweet as
Watermelon

◆ Copy the poem onto the slice by:

Printing the title at the top of the slice.

Printing each of the lines around the red semi-circle so they are spaced in the 3, 6 and 9 o'clock positions.

Printing "Watermelon" in the rind at the bottom.

◆ The words the group chooses to write on the watermelon seeds will complete each of the lines.

◆ Cover the watermelon slice with clear adhesive shelf paper. Display on a bulletin board or easel.

◆ Label each envelope with one of the adjectives: cold, sweet, and heavy.

◆ Enlarge the seed pattern reproducible by doubling the size and then enlarging that seed again, 1.5 times. Cut out nine seeds.

Discussion:

(Ask after reading the book to the children.)

What "word pictures" does the story paint in your mind?

Would you be able to picture the story in your mind without the artist's illustrations?

What do you like about the illustrations for this book?

How do they make you feel?

Library Activity:

(Complete after reading and discussing the book.)

1. Show the children the large watermelon slice and tell them they are going to write a group poem about a watermelon. (The optional watermelon flavored candy should be handed out at this time.)

2. Ask the children to brainstorm words or phrases to describe how cold, heavy and sweet a watermelon is as compared to other things. Think of three words or phrases for each one. For example, the phrases for cold might be: winter wind, ice cream, and a blizzard.

3. Write one word or phrase on each seed with the white correction pen. ("A" or "an" may need to be added before some words.)

4. Place the three seeds with the phrases describing cold in the manila envelope labeled "cold." Do the same for the adjectives "sweet" and "heavy."

5. Let children randomly draw one phrase from each envelope.

6. Roll masking tape to the back of the seed and place it on the watermelon slice with the pointed end toward the title.

7. Read the resulting poem aloud. Ask children to decide if they like the poem or if they would like to try other phrases from the envelopes. Repeat until the class chooses their favorite.

Tech Tie-In:

◆ www.mecca.org/~graham/day/poetrypost

Post the children's poetry online on this Web page link from the Memphis Educational Computer Connectivity Alliance (MECCA) in Memphis, Tennessee. Teachers post the student poetry or have a link to their school Web page. If poetry is posted to the Poetry Post Web page, links to information about the state the student lives in will be available.

Supplies for Classroom Activity:

◆ One paper plate for each child

◆ One watermelon seed reproducible for each child

◆ Crayons

◆ Stapler

◆ Scissors

Preparation for Classroom Activity:

◆ Fold lightweight paper plates in half and cut along the fold.

◆ Staple the curve together near the edge. Leave the straight edge open.

◆ Copy one page of watermelon seeds for each child.

Classroom Activity:

1. Give each child a paper plate watermelon slice and a page of watermelon seeds.

2. Have children print the title and lines on their watermelon slice like the one on the board, except for the last word "Watermelon." Have the children print this in the middle on the other side of the slice.

3. Have children cut out the seeds. Using a white crayon, have them print one word on each seed: 3 for cold, 3 for heavy and 3 for sweet.

4. Have them mix and match their phrases.

5. Children can prepare their slice to return to the classroom by storing the seeds inside the watermelon slice.

6. When they return to their classroom, they can color their watermelon slice lightly on both sides so the printing is visible before they tape the seeds onto the slice.

7. Ask the classroom teacher to display the poetry under the title of "A Taste of Summer."

170

Watermelon Seeds Pattern

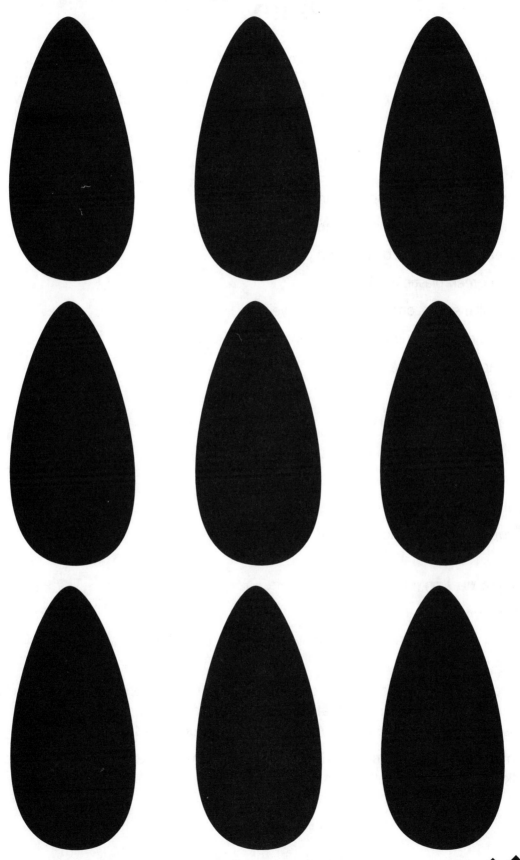

Busy Bee

This simple balloon watermelon will magically grow after a bee pollinates it. Just like a real watermelon, the blossom will fall off after being pollinated by the bee, and the watermelon will begin to grow. With the help of the sun and plenty of rain, it will soon be big enough to pick.

Supplies:

◆ One large (12" diameter) round green balloon

◆ One copy of leaf, blossom and sun pattern reproducible

◆ Green and yellow construction paper

◆ One green plastic drinking straw

◆ Chenille stems, one black and one yellow

◆ 12" pieces of curling ribbon, one yellow and one green

◆ Clear adhesive tape

◆ Scissors

◆ Black permanent marker

◆ Glue stick

◆ Crayons

◆ Glue gun with hot glue

◆ Optional: Watermelon-flavored candy

Preparation:

◆ *Watermelon:*

Trace the sun and blossom patterns on yellow paper. Trace the leaf on green paper. Cut out.

Insert one end of the straw into the opening of the balloon. Tape securely below and above the opening so that no air escapes around the neck of the balloon. The balloon should inflate easily when you blow through the straw.

Inflate the balloon. Draw bold, black lines with the marker to make the balloon look like a watermelon. Let the air out of the balloon.

172

Place the blossom over the end of the balloon farthest from the straw. Only a small part of the green balloon should be visible. Cut the yellow ribbon in half. Fold both pieces together and place at the center of the blossom so the ribbon protrudes like stamens.

Tape the edges of the blossom together to hold it in place.

Tape the leaf to the straw. Tie the green ribbon around the straw above the leaf. Curl it to resemble tendrils.

◆ *Bee:*

Put the yellow and black chenille stems side by side. Wrap both about three times around the tip of your index finger to make the body of the bee.

Carefully remove the coiled black and yellow stems to trim a small piece of the yellow stem so the black stem protrudes. Bend this into a stinger, then cut off the excess and loosely knot it to form the head and antennae of the bee. Hot glue to the bee's body.

Discussion:

(Ask after reading the book to the children.)

What do watermelons grow from? (seeds)

What else grows from seeds?

What part of the watermelon plant turns into a watermelon? (flowers)

Why are bees important to watermelons and people? (pollinate the flowers so the watermelon will grow and people can eat the watermelon)

What will happen to a watermelon plant if the flower doesn't get pollinated? (no watermelon will grow)

What else does a watermelon need to grow? (soil, water and light)

What kind of soil does a watermelon need to grow? (sandy)

What kind of weather? (hot, sunny, rain)

What should not be growing next to the watermelon? (weeds)

Activity:

1. Place the balloon on a flat surface.

2. Choose one child to make the bee fly to the flower and pollinate it by rubbing against the stamens of the flower.

3. Ask one child to pass the picture of the sun over the watermelon.

4. Ask another child to "rain" on the watermelon by wiggling his/her fingers over the watermelon.

   Ask: What do you think will happen next?

5. Slowly blow up the balloon until the blossom falls off. Pinch the end of the straw closed.

6. Build anticipation by repeating steps 3 and 4, inflating the balloon a little more each time.

   Ask: Is it time for a Watermelon Day?

7. Continue until the balloon is fully inflated and the children agree that it is Watermelon Day.

8. Like Pappy in the book, use the side of your fist to hit the watermelon as you let go of the end of the straw to let the air slowly escape.

9. Pass out watermelon candy.

   Ask: How does it compare to Pappy's watermelon?

Tech Tie-In:

◆ www.kathiappelt.com

   Plan a collaborative classroom activity by checking out the author's Web site. Click on Kathi's Classroom Idea Page to find classroom activities for *Watermelon Day* and most of Kathi's other books. Activities are organized by subject.

◆ Plant several watermelon seeds in a small container in the media center. Invite children to take turns tending the crop throughout the season and helping you photograph and record each day's growth to create a watermelon diary.

Leaf, Blossom, and Sun Patterns

Web Sites

The Web sites included in this list are designed to accompany activities in *Read It Again!* They are arranged by grade level and title.

Every effort has been made to select quality Web sites that are likely to be accessible to the reader for years to come. However, all users of this book are strongly advised to check Web sites before planning any activities. This list is designed to simplify checking on the current status of any of the Web sites selected.

Pre-K Titles:

Here Comes Mother Goose
http://www.librarysupport.net/mothergoosesociety/

Little Cloud
http://www.reachoutmichigan.org/funexperiments/quick/raincloud.html

Who Hoots?
http://www.wildsanctuary.com/safari.html

Kindergarten Titles:

Baby Duck and the Bad Eyeglasses
http://www.dada.it/eyeweb/ealbin.htm

Bark, George
http://www.ci.shrewsbury.ma.us/Sps/Schools/Beal/Curriculum/critterclinic/critterclinic.html
http://www.uga.edu/~lam/kids/

Gregory the Terrible Eater
http://www.childrenssoftware.com/lc/funfood
http://www.usda.gov/cnpp/KidsPyra/

Make Way for Ducklings
http://www.inspiration.com

Max Cleans Up
http://www.rosemarywells.com

Red-Eyed Tree Frog
http://www.pbs.org/tal/costa_rica/rainwalk.html

The Very Clumsy Click Beetle
http://bugscope.beckman.uiuc.edu

Early Elementary Titles:

Come On, Rain!
http://www.wunderground.com

Good Night, Good Knight
http://www.yourchildlearns.com/heraldry.htm

Jamela's Dress
http://www.countryreports.org
http://ipl.si.umich.edu/div/kidspace/cquest/
http://www.pics4learning.com

Jingle Dancer
http://www.cynthialeitichsmith.com/jingledancerlinks.htm

Joseph Had a Little Overcoat
http://www.ibiblio.org/yiddish/school.html/

Mike Mulligan and His Steam Shovel
http://StarChild.gsfc.nasa.gov

My Very Own Room
http://www.littleexplorers.com/languages/Spanishdictionary.html

Silver Seeds
http://www.geocities.com/EnchantedForest/5165/pages/acrostic.html

Watermelon Day
http://www.mecca.org/~graham/day/poetrypost
http://www.kathiappelt.com

Key to Standards Cited in *Read It Again!*

Standard	Topic/Discipline	Organization/Standards Link
AAHE	Health	American Association for Health Education www.mcrel.org
ALA	Information Literacy	American Library Association www.ala.org/aasl/ip_nine.html
ISTE	Technology	International Society for Technology in Education www.iste.org
MENC	Arts	Music Educators National Conference www.artsedge.kennedy-center.org
NAS	Science	National Academy of Sciences htpp://books.nap.edu/html/nses/html/6c.html
NASPE	Physical Education	National Association for Sport and Physical Education www.mcrel.org
NCEE	Economics	National Council on Economic Education www.economicsamerica.org/standards/
NCHS	History	National Center for History in the Schools www.sscnet.ucla.edu/nchs/standards
NCTE	English	National Council of Teachers of English www.ncte.org/standards
NCTM	Mathematics	National Council of Teachers of Mathematics www.nctm.org/standards
NGS	Geography	National Geography Standards www.nationalgeographic.com/xpeditions/standards

For a complete listing of National Standards and a searchable K–12 compendium, log onto **www.mcrel.org**.

Print Bibliography

Activities are included for each of the thirty titles in this bibliography. Complete annotations can be found with the Skills Table for each title.

Preschool Titles:

Baker, Keith, *Quack and Count*. Harcourt Brace, 1999, 20 pp., 0-15-292858-8

Blos, Joan, *Hello, Shoes!* Simon and Schuster Books for Young Readers, 1999, 24 pp., 0-689-81441-0

Carle, Eric, *Little Cloud*. Philomel, 1996, 26 pp., 0-399-23034-5

Davis, Katie, *Who Hoots?* Harcourt, 2000, 36 pp., 0-15-202312-7

Fleming, Denise, *In the Tall, Tall Grass*. H. Holt, 1991, 32 pp., 0-8050-1635-X

Here Comes Mother Goose. Edited by Iona Opie. Candlewick Press, 1999, 107 pp., 0-7636-0683-9

Keats, Ezra Jack, *The Snowy Day*. Viking Press, 1962, 32pp., 0-670-65400-0

Sis, Peter, *Trucks, Trucks, Trucks*. Greenwillow Books, 1999, 24 pp., 0-688-16276-2

Tafuri, Nancy, *What the Sun Sees, What the Moon Sees*. Greenwillow Books, 1997, 32 pp., 0-688-14494-2

Walsh, Ellen Stohl, *Mouse Count*. Harcourt Brace, 1991, 32 pp., 0-15-256023-8

Kindergarten Titles:

Carle, Eric, *The Very Clumsy Click Beetle*. Philomel, 1999, 26 pp., 0-399-23201-X

Cowley, Joy, *Red-Eyed Tree Frog*. Scholastic, 1999, 32 pp., 0-590-87175-7

Ehlert, Lois, *Red Leaf, Yellow Leaf*. Harcourt Brace, 1991, 36 pp., 0-15-266197-2

Feiffer, Jules, *Bark, George*. HarperCollins, 1999, 32 pp., 0-06-205185-7

Freeman, Don, *A Pocket for Corduroy*. Viking, 1978, 32 pp., 0-670-56172-X

Hest, Amy, *Baby Duck and the Bad Eyeglasses*. Candlewick Press, 1996, 28 pp., 1-56402-680-9

Keller, Holly, *That's Mine Horace*. Greenwillow Books, 2000, 24 pp., 0-688-17160-5

McCloskey, Robert, *Make Way for Ducklings*. Viking, 1941, 65 pp., 0-670-45149-5

Sharmat, Mitchell, *Gregory the Terrible Eater*. Scholastic, 1980, 32 pp., 0-590-07586-1

Wells, Rosemary, *Max Cleans Up*. Viking, 2000, 24 pp., 0-0670-89218-1

Early Elementary Titles:

Appelt, Kathi, *Watermelon Day*. H. Holt, 1994, 34 pp., 0-8050-2304-6

Burton, Virginia Lee, *Mike Mulligan and His Steam Shovel*. Houghton Mifflin, 1967, 44 pp., 0-395-16961-5

Daly, Niki, *Jamela's Dress*. Farrar, Straus & Giroux, 1999, 31 pp., 0-374-33667-9

French, Vivian, *Growing Frogs.* Candlewick Press, 2000, 30 pp., 0-7636-0317-1

Hesse, Karen, *Come On Rain!,* Scholastic, 1999, 32 pp., 0-590-33125-6

Paolilli, Paul and Brewer, Dan, *Silver Seeds*. Viking, 2001, 32 pp., 0-670-88941-5

Perez, Amada Irma, *My Very Own Room*. Children's Book Press, 2000, 32 pp., 0-89239-164-2

Smith, Cynthia Leitich, *Jingle Dancer*. Morrow Junior Books, 2000, 32 pp., 0-688-16242-8

Taback, Simms, *Joseph Had a Little Overcoat*. Viking, 1999, 36 pp., 0-670-87855-3

Thomas, Shelley Moore, *Good Night, Good Knight*. Dutton, 2000, 47 pp., 0-525-46326-7

180

Non-Print Bibliography

Videocassette:

Ezra Jack Keats Video Library. 1996. 37 min. Weston Woods.
   (265 Post Road West, Westport, CT 06880)

In the Tall Tall Grass. 1992. 6 minutes. Spoken Arts.
   (P.O. Box 100, New Rochelle, NY 10802)

Into the Circle. 1992. 58 min. Full Circle Communications.
   (1131 S. College Ave., Tulsa, OK 74104)

Joseph Had a Little Overcoat. 2001. 10 minutes. Includes teachers guide.
   Weston Woods. (265 Post Road West, Westport, CT 06880)

Mike Mulligan and his Steam Shovel Videorecording: The Musical. 1991. 30 min.
   Includes study guide. Ambrose Video Publication, Inc.
   (145 W. 45th St., Suite 1115, New York, NY 10036)

A Pocket for Corduroy. 1986. 20 minutes. Phoenix/BFA Films and Video, Inc.
   (470 Park Ave. South, New York, NY 10016)

Road Construction Ahead. 1991. 30 minutes. Fred Levine Productions.
   (64 Main St., Suite 26, Montpelier, VT 05602)

CD and Audiocassette:

All of the following titles are available on CD or cassette.

Castles, Knights & Unicorns. Ronno, 2001. Kimbo Educational.
   (P.O. Box 477, Long Branch, NJ 07740)

Nursery Rhyme Time. Georgiana Stewart, 2000. Includes guide with lyrics/activities.
   Kimbo Educational. (P.O. Box 477, Long Branch, NJ 07740)

Sing a Song of Seasons. Rachel Buchman, 1997. Rounder Records Corp.
   (1 Camp Street, Cambridge, MA 02140)

Weather. Kim Mitzo Thompson and Karen Mitzo Hildenbrand, 1999. An activity book is
   available. Twin Sister Productions, Inc. (2680 West Market St., Akron, OH 44333)

Software:

Build a Math Bug. 1999. Win/Mac. Edmark.
   (6727 185th Ave. NE. Redmond, WA 98073)

Mike Mulligan and His Steam Shovel. 1996. WIN/MAC. Houghton Mifflin
   Interactive/Sunburst Technology. (1900 S. Batavia Ave., Geneva, IL 60134)

Millie's Math House. 1995. Win/Mac. Edmark.
   (6727 185th Ave. NE. Redmond, WA 98073)

About the Author

Linda Ayers is an elementary school librarian in Mabank, Texas, where she continues to share the best of children's literature with her students. She has taught preschool, kindergarten and second grade children and worked as a public library outreach coordinator. A certified Big6™ Texas Trainer of Trainers, she advocates for the importance of literature activities through her writing and workshop presentations.

Linda received her Bachelor's degree from Oklahoma State University with majors in Family Relations and Child Development. She lives in the piney woods of East Texas with her husband, two sons, and a menagerie of pets. When she is not working or planning activities, she likes to camp with her family, create various crafts, write fiction and poetry, and of course, read.